Free Agency

Richard Templar

- Fast track route to making the most of working solo

- Covers all the key aspects of free agency, from finding and using business advice to researching the market for your skills, and from managing your cash flow to selling yourself

- Packed with lessons and tips from people who have successfully jumped the corporate ship and made rewarding independent careers

- Includes a glossary of key concepts and a comprehensive resources guide

>>EXPRESS EXEC.COM<<
essential management thinking at your fingertips

LIFE & WORK

10.08

First published 2002 by
Capstone Publishing (a Wiley company)
8 Newtec Place
Magdalen Road
Oxford OX4 1RE
United Kingdom
http://www.capstoneideas.com

CIP catalogue records for this book are available from the British Library and the US Library of Congress

ISBN 1-84112-309-9

Printed and bound in Great Britain

This book is printed on acid-free paper

Substantial discounts on bulk quantities of Capstone books are available to corporations, professional associations and other organizations. Please contact Capstone for more details on +44 (0)1865 798 623 or (fax) +44 (0)1865 240 941 or (e-mail) info@wiley-capstone.co.uk

Contents

Introduction to ExpressExec

ExpressExec is 3 million words of the latest management thinking compiled into 10 modules. Each module contains 10 individual titles forming a comprehensive resource of current business practice written by leading practitioners in their field. From brand management to balanced scorecard, ExpressExec enables you to grasp the key concepts behind each subject and implement the theory immediately. Each of the 100 titles is available in print and electronic formats.

Through the ExpressExec.com Website you will discover that you can access the complete resource in a number of ways:

» printed books or e-books;
» e-content – PDF or XML (for licensed syndication) adding value to an intranet or Internet site;
» a corporate e-learning/knowledge management solution providing a cost-effective platform for developing skills and sharing knowledge within an organization;
» bespoke delivery – tailored solutions to solve your need.

Why not visit www.expressexec.com and register for free key management briefings, a monthly newsletter and interactive skills checklists. Share your ideas about ExpressExec and your thoughts about business today.

Please contact elound@wiley-capstone.co.uk for more information.

Introduction to Free Agency

What exactly is free agency? How does a free agent differ from a freelance? This chapter considers the changing nature of free agents in a modern business world.

- » Rise of free agency
- » What it means
- » Statistics for growth in number of free agents
- » Factors driving the shift
- » Rise of individualism
- » Social and economic context
- » Why work for an organization when you can work for yourself?
- » Are free agents any happier?
- » Being responsible for career
- » Can corporations accommodate free agents?
- » The new challenges

"My professional independence means I love what I do, do what I love, and never wear pantyhose or hairspray again."

Elaine Biech, president of the management consulting firm Ebb Associates in Portage, Wisconsin, author of The Consultant's Quick Start Guide: An Action Plan for Your First Year in Business

RISE OF FREE AGENCY

Our knowledge is constantly changing – and expanding. The sum of all human knowledge is now so great that it can no longer be recorded in one place or in one format or indeed even stored in one country. No one human being can learn more than the merest fraction of that sum of human knowledge.

As managers we cannot know everything – that's not our job. But when we want something done we need to know who to call in to get that job done – that is our role: the facilitator. The free agent is the person with that bit of specialist knowledge that we need. We want them to come in, do the job and go. We don't need them as full-time employees. We don't need them to stick around and monitor things, our own people can do that. We just want them to bridge the gap in our own knowledge and not hang around afterwards. These are the free agents.

WHAT IT MEANS

So who are these free agents and what do they do? Well, we might all be using different words to describe them – consultants, independent professionals, e-lancers, freelancers – but they all pretty well conform to a norm. They are the professionals who have left the safe haven of the corporation on a mission of their own to search out a more rewarding and enriching (both financially and job satisfaction-wise) career as a self-employed independent professional. They are the free agents.

STATISTICS FOR GROWTH IN NUMBER OF FREE AGENTS

The rise in the number of free agents is staggering. The US Department of Labor reckons there are just under 9 million people who identify themselves as free agents in America but that figure may be much higher – as high as 30 million – because of the problems of specifically defining the terminology. What one calls a free agent another may call a self-employed business person and a third may call a freelance consultant.

If you band together all the workers under their separate banners of self-employed, freelance, independent professional, consultant, contract worker, on-call worker, free agent, and such like, the resulting statistic may well show that around 25% of all workers in America are actually free agents of some sort or another.

FACTORS DRIVING THE SHIFT

But whatever they are called, the trend is gaining momentum. The reasons for this we will look at in more detail later, but for the moment it is sufficient to say that it a combination of factors including:

» the impact of new technology;
» people's desire for increased personal choice in their working practices;
» downsizing; and
» the revolution in the jobs-for-life scenario.

Moreover, it seems that corporations are as anxious as individuals to capitalize on this growing trend, as it allows them to bring in experts on a short-term fixed contract basis – bridging the ignorance gap – and thus avoiding the usual costs associated with hiring, recruiting, and training full-time members of staff.

RISE OF INDIVIDUALISM

Henry Ford certainly knew how to make the best use of his workforce. He understood the need to organize large pools of labor so that mass production could be effective and efficient. And for a long while we went along with it. We were happy to be sheep – albeit well looked after and well nurtured, but sheep nevertheless. But not any more. Henry Ford and his ilk represented the pinnacle of the industrial revolution. But in enslaving us in mass production he also sowed the seeds of freedom. Once you have workers in such vast numbers you have to set up a caring environment for them – pay them well, organize social events, implement pensions, and the like. Ford paid his workers more than the going rate, both to keep them and to make sure they could afford to buy one of the cars they were making – clever, isn't it? As soon as they were well paid these workers could afford better education for their own children and the revolution in our working habits was under way.

SOCIAL AND ECONOMIC CONTEXT

So now we are better educated. We expect more from life and work than mere drudgery and boredom. We want to be challenged, stimulated, motivated, interested, and most importantly, given free choice over our working lives. We no longer expect jobs-for-life – indeed the concept is now considered so abhorrent that entire recessions can be traced to the inability of the workforce to embark on this new working revolution. You only have to consider Japan and its shrinking and tattered economy of late to realize that mass production using an automated workforce no longer works. Japan has seen monumental lay-offs because its workers' mentality hasn't been able to shift into this new dimension as quickly as Western economies. Of course, now the problem is extreme they are countering with quality circles and suggestion schemes.

Companies now expect their workforce to be creative and flexible, fluid, and able to adjust rapidly and efficiently to new working practices and trends. Gone are the days of structured autonomy and rigid thinking. We all have to adapt fast to survive.

WHY WORK FOR AN ORGANIZATION WHEN YOU CAN WORK FOR YOURSELF?

Previously we looked at how the sum of human knowledge has grown too large to handle. Once you have that volume of knowledge you create niches for the specialist – the person who can capitalize on their knowledge and sell it to the highest bidder. They no longer need to put up with the routine of a 9 to 5 but can set their own agenda. They can choose when and where they work. And most corporations have enough savvy to recognize that it is in their own financial best interest not to have a captive workforce any more but to hire as and when they need a specialist to bridge their ignorance gap.

We are now all mostly well educated and intelligent and we demand more from our working life. Why work for a corporation when a free agent can work for themselves? The answer to most of them is pretty obvious. It frees them to enjoy their work more. It presents them with the challenge of selling their services. It stimulates them and keeps them on their toes. And most importantly it offers them the opportunity to earn more and be more satisfied. And are they?

ARE FREE AGENTS ANY HAPPIER?

It seems they are. Recent research conducted in the US indicates that some 70% of free agents report that they are *very* satisfied with their work. This compares with around 50% of full-time employees. It would appear that when they are happy with their work they are very happy.

Around 35% of full-time workers claim to be just about OK with their work, somewhat satisfied but not shouting for joy particularly. But only about 25% of free agents claimed to be in the same category. Free agents would appear to be achieving their aims – more satisfaction indeed.

BEING RESPONSIBLE FOR CAREER

One of the reasons for the enhanced satisfaction is that free agents feel more in control of their careers. They have the necessary drive and determination to advance themselves independently. They aren't subject to random promotion or the tricky selection interview process. They sell their talents and by improving those talents and skills they progress. It is in their own hands to do better, earn more, move on up. Obviously, to be successful they have to recognize that there are skills beyond their work discipline to take on board and acquire. They may be a brilliant engineer or a first class programmer but they will still need to:

» be good at promoting and marketing their services;
» have a proven record of success and experience;
» enjoy working independently;

» be able to deal with the clerical, billing and accounting side of their business;
» be able to handle their own benefit packages including pensions and health care;
» be self-motivating;
» be able to handle the high risk being a free agent entails, with its risk of non-employment at times;
» plan and be able to undertake training to keep their skills up to date; and
» have a strong network of contacts.

It's a tall order but the challenge is sufficient to encourage more and more people to take the plunge and become free agents.

CAN CORPORATIONS ACCOMMODATE FREE AGENTS?

They have to if they are to survive in this day and age. The new workforce is mobile and specialist. Corporations have to cut their costs to the bone and the biggest cost to most corporations is their staffing. If they can cut their workforce to the barest minimum and use free agents on short-term contacts to bridge the ignorance gap, they become sleeker and more profitable. Microsoft uses many more free agents than full-time workers for just these reasons – and Microsoft is so sleek and profitable it has attracted more than its fair share of attention.

Work in IT is now so large that most corporations are engaged in some way or another with it. They need a workforce which is computer literate and Internet experienced. Once you begin to make profits from IT, it quickly becomes apparent that the old dogmas of a static workforce are redundant. If you don't have to have them in the office – indeed don't have to have the office itself any more – then you don't need to have a workforce either. You can pick the best of what is on offer and only pay for what you use.

THE NEW CHALLENGES

The demand for free agents is increasing, as is the oxygen of their existence – they become self-perpetuating. But where do we go from here? Will we all become teleworkers? Apparently not. It would seem that the revolution has come full circle and that workers are now beginning to feel the need to draw closer to other people again. We are social animals and need to interact and communicate one-to-one, face on. We need the social activity of an office staffed with other people. Teleworkers complain of feelings of isolation and withdrawal. The new challenge for corporations is to accommodate the free agents within a social work situation. And the challenge for the free agents is to work socially and still be independent and flexible. No one wants a return to the old office situation of a few years ago where we were mentally tied to our desk, but nor, it seems, do we want to work in isolation and obscurity. We want to meet with our fellow workers but not be tied down. In Chapter 7 we will look at several success stories where corporations have risen effectively to meet these challenges head on.

What is Free Agency?

How do we define a free agent? How do we see individuals who work for companies but are still entrepreneurs? This chapter examines exactly what makes a free agent a free agent.

- » What is free agency?
- » The free agent as entrepreneur
- » Bruce Tulgan
- » Dan Pink
- » Free agents and the law

"Free agents are a special breed, committed to independence as a career choice, thriving on challenge and deriving their job satisfaction from resolving problems."

Personnel Today (October 2000)

WHAT IS FREE AGENCY?

When armies clashed in the mediaeval period they obviously used conscripted peasants as the main thrust of their attacks. But these press-ganged laborers, farm workers and untrained soldiers were ineffective at times and rather fearful. Army commanders sought better fighters. Enter the era of the jousting mercenaries – they sold their services to the highest bidder, were trained and effective, and would fight successfully and bravely. As jousting knights they used the lance as their favorite weapon.

That's where we get the term *freelance*. Now wind forward to today. We have our freelances – your local plumber is one; I, as a writer, am one. The freelances sell their services to whoever needs them. They are project-based in the sense that they work on a single project for a company (or individual) and then move on to their next project. They deal with their own tax affairs and could not be misinterpreted as an employee. They supply their own tools of the trade and work for several, if not many, different companies. And within those companies there may be people who have specialist knowledge and who are regarded as employees.

Suppose these employees realize that their talents and skills could be offered to several companies. Why then, they leave the cosy environment of employment and strike out on their own, selling their services much like your local plumber does. The main difference is that they choose to style themselves free agents rather than freelancers. And they sell their time, skills and talents rather than a specific project. They are time- or project-led rather than task-led.

Suppose you are a local government department in charge of roads and their upkeep. It is reported to you that a bridge on the main road into town is defective and possibly weak. There isn't a trade that operates as a freelance one that you can call in. Your local plumber can't handle this. Nor can your full-time employees. This is a specialist job requiring specialist talents. You call in the free agents who hopefully, like white knights, will ride to your rescue. They may be there some time while a report into the bridge's structure is commissioned, and then there may well be lots of them while the bridge is strengthened or whatever it needs. Then they will be gone again because their job isn't long-term – they do repairs but not day-to-day maintenance. They are the Lone Rangers of the business world.

In the UK this was always known as "hump" management – you called in the specialists to get you over a specific hump or problem.

The term *free agent* is taken from the world of sport. In American football, basketball, and baseball – amongst many others – sports people are contracted to work (provide their services) for a particular club for a period of years. Once they have served their fixed term they can become free agents. Technically, they are still contracted to their club but on short-term contracts. They are free to leave whenever they want and to sign for another club. Maybe in a few years we might see a sporting star contracted for a particular match or game only and not for a period of time. Thus a sports person could be employed for perhaps an hour and a half only and then be free to move to another venue or club.

The status of free agency varies according to the sport, and details for each of the four major leagues in the US are shown below.

» **Baseball** – a player can become a free agent after completing six years of service.
» **Football** – any player who has completed five years in a non-salary capped year and four years in a salary capped year. A class of restricted free agents (requiring compensation from the team which signed the player) exists for those players who have played three or more seasons.
» **Basketball** – any player who has completed five years. In basketball it used to be only three years but it has been brought in line with the other major leagues.
» **Hockey** – any player who has completed four seasons and is over 31 years old. Younger players can join the ranks of restricted free agents with compensation required.

And there are varying forms of free agency within the sporting world.

» **UFA** – an Unrestricted Free Agent, a player with four or more years' experience, who can sign with any team, including their own, with no compensation involved.
» **RFA** – a Restricted Free Agent, a player with three years' experience. Teams have the right to match any offer made to their restricted players and are entitled to draft choices as compensation if they choose not to match, provided the team has made the appropriate qualifying offer.
» **TFA** – a Transition Free Agent, a player who can negotiate with any club but whose current team retains matching rights.
» **FFA** – a Franchise Free Agent, a player who may negotiate with other clubs, but whose original club reserves the right to match any offer, or refuse to match it and receive two first-round draft picks as compensation.

This terminology has extended to the business world as well – see the glossary of free agency terms in Chapter 8.

THE FREE AGENT AS ENTREPRENEUR

So what does the individual offer that an employee can't? Well, for a start a company doesn't want these people on the payroll. It's simply too expensive to employ specialists just in case they are needed. It is also a waste of their time and creativity to be thus employed. The one thing all free agents seem to have in common is their creative need to be an entrepreneur. They like the challenge of selling their services – in fact some of them may well think of themselves as the white knights of business. They have a role as troubleshooters and problem solvers. They are versatile and adaptable. For them, the boredom of full-time employment is an anathema. They may well work on a particular site for more than six months – in some cases as long as three years – but they know the contract is limited, it will come to an end, and they can be off again in search of new challenges, new tasks, new horizons.

A recent survey in America threw up some interesting results on this theme.

» Some 80% of free agents said they preferred to remain independent and said that they enjoyed the freedom and flexibility of controlling their careers.

» No matter in what industry they worked, the 70% figure we looked at in Chapter 1 remained constant. Whether they were engineers, computer programmers, legal consultants, financial planners, or whatever. The industry was irrelevant, the status as a free agent was important.

» 95% of all free agents interviewed said they were confident of being able to earn a reasonable living over the next five years.

» Free agents are twice as likely to earn in excess of $75,000 when compared to their employed contemporaries.

But to be a free agent the person has to know both their strengths and limitations – it ain't for everyone. As a free agent there has to be both an element of the entrepreneur and the risk taker. Specific skills are involved, such as:

» offering technical assistance such as programming, designing, writing, etc.;
» identifying problems;
» solving problems;
» generating new ideas and processes;
» identifying growth areas;
» recognizing strategic opportunities;
» providing expert knowledge;
» teaching new methodologies;
» training in new procedures;
» relevant outsourcing functions; and
» providing support and backup during peak periods.

BRUCE TULGAN

Who dragged the free agents from the sporting world into the business world? Well, a lot of the credit can go to Bruce Tulgan who wrote *Managing Generation X* in the mid-nineties. In this he suggested – and stunned the business management world – that the stubborn independence of young workers would be more than a temporary blip and that the effects of this new mobile workforce would be dramatic and revolutionary. It would actually be the first salvo in a fierce battle between the traditional worker and the management. Since then free agency has swept the business world and forced a great many business leaders to completely rethink their strategy for hiring their workers. His philosophy, which has now been taken on board by progressive and successful companies, is to staff the work, not the job, and to pay people when they deliver the goods.

He suggests that retention is no longer the best policy but rather that fluidity is – employ the creative people as and when they are needed and utilize their talents and their restless independence. By not hemming in workers you can get more out of them – hence the *free* part of free agency.

DAN PINK

The editor of *FreeAgent.com* (see Chapter 9), Dan Pink, says that being a free agent isn't all laughs – but it should be fun. And he ought to know. Just before becoming a free agent himself he was Al Gore's chief speech writer and his articles about the new economy have appeared in *The New York Times*, *The Washington Post*, *The Worldly Investor* and *Fast Company*. As well as being the editor-at-large for *FreeAgent.com*, he also produces the Website FreeAgentNation.com.

> "Leaving the corporate world for free agency isn't quite on the same moral plane as breaking free of an imperialist power that crushed religious freedom and taxed people without giving them the full rights of citizenship. But for me, the animating ideals were remarkably similar – life, liberty, and the pursuit of happiness."
> *Dan Pink, free agent guru based in Washington, DC, author of*
> Free Agent Nation: How America's New Independent
> Workers Are Transforming the Way We Live

FREE AGENTS AND THE LAW

What we might define as a free agent and what the IRS defines can be two different things, and this is worth bearing in mind if individuals or corporations don't want to run foul of the tax laws. In the UK this issue is currently causing considerable problems. Free agents, who up until now have considered themselves as independent consultants, are now being pursued by the Inland Revenue under IR35, a new directive which changes their job status to that of full-time employee. There has been one recent test case – the Professional Contractors' Group (PCG) lost their battle – where the judgement was awarded in favor of the Inland Revenue with the proviso that they went away and drew up a more specific set of rules to define both the free agent and the full-time employee. At the current time of writing a definitive document is still awaited.

The High Court in London ruled that the IR35 legislation did not breach European law and the Human Rights Act. The situation in Europe remains unaffected, and free agents can continue to operate freely.

In the US a similar action was brought by the IRS against Microsoft for their federal payroll tax accounts for 1989 and 1990. It was deemed that Microsoft had to reclassify its free agents as traditional employees for tax purposes. The ruling cost Microsoft several millions of dollars in back taxes and benefit reimbursements. And because of this ruling many free agents have been scared off. They have been forced to take full-time employment rather than face the risk of being penalized for back taxes. But some enterprising free agents are getting round this, however, by using staffing agencies. These agencies, in practice, employ the free agents and then subcontract them to the corporations.

In most cases the tax situation is muddied. There is no clear definition of what constitutes a free agent. The following recommendations are given, but only by a free agent talking directly to their tax advisor can a clear position be reached.

» Ensure it is obvious that an independence of the corporation is in force.
» Do not become part of any employment review system.
» Make sure it is clear that the free agent is free to work their own hours and doesn't have to "clock in."
» Operate from own premises wherever possible.
» Have a formal invoicing system set up and don't go on a payroll.
» Make sure that there is independence of other staff, and refuse to accept responsibility for full-time workers.

» Do not accept a company car or use cars from a company pool.
» Make sure that there are independent business cards and letterheads.
» Be responsible for personal pension and insurance payments.
» Make sure there is a registration for VAT (UK and Europe).
» Make sure there is a clear contract which specifies the task responsibilities – and adhere to it. Do not agree to any tasks outside of the scope of the contract.

None of the above is guaranteed to avoid IR35 (UK) or IRS 1706 (US) but it does go a long way to presenting a decent case for being classified as a free agent rather than a full-time worker.

One test the IRS in the US use is what it calls "right of control." By this it means: what control does a free agent have to decide:

» where they work?
» when they work?
» how they work?

If they have pretty well complete independence over these three criteria then they are deemed to be free agents. If, however, they do not have control over these areas then they are considered to be employees.

This problem with classification has led to the setting up of numerous free agents' agencies. These aren't, of course, free but charge a percentage on the free agent's charges to the corporation. For the free agent these free agencies provide a measure of security by:

» offering liability protection from the IRS 1706 ruling such as the case against Microsoft;
» being responsible for the paperwork side of the free agent's business, such as invoicing;
» providing pension and benefit packages including 401 (k) tax-deferred; and
» matching free agents with relevant opportunities with corporations.

As the free agent is technically employed by the free agency their work record remains continuous even if they have periods when they do not work. This can help the look of the resume, with no blanks for long periods of unemployment.

The other option for free agents is to set up their own limited company for which they work and then they sell their services to that company, which in turn sells them on to corporations. In the UK this situation is being closely monitored by the Inland Revenue, which says that free agents running personal service companies pay less tax than normal employees because they are able to pay their salaries as dividends and store up profits to engineer favorable capital gains tax outcomes. They also avoid paying National Insurance surcharges on profits. They are currently redefining many consultants as workers for tax purposes and claim that they may be able to recoup some $500mn in tax (around £350mn) and that they are gunning for some 90,000 free agents.

So defining what is and what isn't a free agent is complex and unclear. The free agent may be certain in their own mind that they are independent and free but come up against a completely different assessment from their tax office.

LEARNING POINTS

» Hump management.
» UFA.
» RFA.
» TFA.
» FFA.
» Bruce Tulgan.
» Dan Pink.
» IR35.
» IRS 1706.
» Personal services companies.

The Evolution of the Free Agent

So how did we get to where we are today? What are the factors in the workplace which led to the evolution of the free agent? This chapter considers the history and development of the free agent.

» Short history of free agencies
» How we got to where we are now
» The shift to self-employment
» Changing employment landscapes
» The end of jobs-for-life
» Widespread downsizing
» The rise of the knowledge workers
» Employer loyalty and its demise
» The end of psychological contracts
» The move to short-term contracts
» The change in attitudes to employment

"When you work, you sell off units of your life called hours in return for units of freedom called dollars. Professional independence allows you to control the ratio of life you sell for liberty, and therefore achieve a more perfect balance in your pursuit of happiness."

Matthew Strebe, owner of Connetic, a network integration firm in San Diego, author of From Serf to Surfer: Becoming a Network Consultant

SHORT HISTORY OF FREE AGENCIES

Being a free agent is a new phenomenon but it is also a very old and traditional career choice. We all use new terminology and new buzz words to try to stay ahead of the game and "free agent" is just another way of saying consultant or independent professional. But being a free agent is evolving. Owing to the massive world recessions of the seventies and early nineties, things in the business world have changed dramatically. Huge lay-offs and downsizing have contributed greatly to a more mobile workforce. If the corporations have proved that they have no staff loyalty – in the event of a recession they think nothing of laying off staff – then the workforce has been obliged to reconsider its own working practices. No longer are workers prepared to put up and shut up. Instead they seek greater autonomy and a wider independence.

The old fashioned company approach was based on a parent/child relationship. The company provided the framework of parent and told the workers – the children in the equation – what they should do and when they should do it. The workers occasionally rebelled and threw tantrums which were known as industrial actions. But the long and short of it was that the relationship was unequal and unfair. The companies reaped the profits while the workers slaved for a pittance. Workers often worked their entire working life without ever getting ahead and retired worn out and broken, whereas the company owner did very nicely, thank you. Consider for a moment the case of John Rockefeller who controlled the giant corporation, Standard Oil. Not only was he the world's first billionaire, he was for quite a time the world's *only* billionaire. At the height of his fortune he was worth $9bn. Consider the humble oilman who worked for him. Do you think they ever got their head above water? I doubt it.

Now consider Bill Gates, who heads Microsoft. A similar success story, but Mr Gates likes to use free agents – independent programmers. These work on extremely high remuneration packages and Bill is fond of saying "we don't have a problem with staff phoning in sick, we have a problem with staff phoning in rich." Microsoft pioneered the practice of offering stock options to all its workers. This has made millionaires out of literally thousands of Microsoft employees, and billionaires out of some of them.

So how has this revolution in worker/company relationships been achieved?

HOW WE GOT TO WHERE WE ARE NOW

Once there was a rural economy based on growing stuff and selling it through markets and on to suppliers. There were peasants and landowners. Then we had the industrial revolution, when cheap coal and new-fangled engines led many workers to abandon the countryside and move to the cities and industrial areas to seek more prosperous work.

For a while these workers were happy to enjoy their new found wealth gained from working in factories and industrial units. The companies that employed them also benefitted, and great wealth was amassed by some individuals – but not the workers. They may have earned a wage but they weren't getting their head above water. The truth of it is that they had nothing to sell apart from their sweat, and that was a commodity in easy supply. The land wasn't supporting too many itinerant workers because tractors, the threshing machines, and combine harvesters had replaced them. More and more unskilled laborers flocked to the cities, driving wages down and company malpractice up. You could afford to be cavalier with your workforce if they could all be replaced.

THE SHIFT TO SELF-EMPLOYMENT

During the twentieth century there were two cataclysmic world wars, which had far-reaching effects on employment and the role of the worker. Basically and in simple language, men went off to fight and women took their place in the factories and on the production line.

There is no right or wrong in this – it is the way it happened. Women discovered a new independence and a life outside and beyond the home. This happened in both wars, although to a much greater extent in the second one.

When the men returned home they found two things waiting for them:

» women were reluctant to give up this new independence; and
» there had been revolution in production processes and technology while they had been away.

The effort needed to produce enough armaments and machinery during the war had led to a massive rethink in production methods. A lot of men returned to find themselves out of a job because they were no longer skilled enough. The women didn't want to return to their old roles as mothers and housewives. There was a lot of unemployment in America after the war but not massive deprivation because the women were still capable of earning a living. The men sought to redress the balance by starting their own businesses to:

» earn independent money and not wait for handouts from their wives;
» restore their lost dignity and pride; and
» carry on exercising a measure of independence for themselves, which they had discovered to a certain degree while away fighting.

Men, in short, had a revolution thrust upon them. Of course, this didn't happen to everyone – but it did happen to a significant proportion, who were then the spearhead of a new order, a new way of looking at employment. The fathers set examples their sons and daughters wouldn't be slow to capitalize on in later decades of the twentieth century.

CHANGING EMPLOYMENT LANDSCAPES

If you watch old newsreels of life before about 1964 it is all in black and white – and gray. But something happened in the early sixties that changed a lot of people's thinking. It has been blamed (or attributed) to radiation in school milk from the Hiroshima fallout affecting the post-war babies who would go on to head the hippie revolution;

sunspots; an end to rationing; free vitamins; improved vaccination techniques; a genetic change of direction; Roswell; add your own theory here. Whatever. There is no doubt that there was a radical and dramatic shift in people's thinking in the sixties. In the West we had the hippie era, which was all about freedom and independence, whereas the East went for repression and suppression. These perhaps were both extremes but interesting as sociological developments nonetheless. Is it not fascinating that in 1961 the West was watching the Dick van Dyke show and swooning to Elvis singing "Are you lonesome tonight?" while in Berlin the wall was going up? And in 1963 we had Bobby Vee and "The night has a thousand eyes" while in the USSR they were detonating a 50-megaton hydrogen bomb in the largest deliberate explosion in history. In the same year John F Kennedy visited Berlin and declared "Ich bin ein Berliner" (I am a Berliner – or I am a jelly doughnut according to some sources) and here in the West we danced to the new music of a funny little band called The Beatles. Things were changing, things were happening.

THE END OF JOBS-FOR-LIFE

As the sixties drew to a close, students in France took up arms against the establishment, as did students in the US (protesting against the Vietnam War – or was it just Nixon? – which wouldn't end until 1975) and elsewhere. New industries were springing up but the new graduates wanted a different working relationship. They wanted casual dress and their creativity recognized. They wanted freedoms and benefits previously unheard of. And the corporations were more than happy to accommodate them. They too sought change and revolution. They sought to reduce their vast workforces because new technologies were making it possible to do more with less people. The car industries in the sixties and seventies saw massive lay-offs as robotic technology replaced human resources. No longer could anyone be confident of a job-for-life and – what is probably more important – no one wanted such a thing. We had all grown up and wanted freedom and creativity and independence in our working life. Enter stage left The Computer, which would aid and abet us all to freedom.

WIDESPREAD DOWNSIZING

In the eighties the buzz word was "downsizing". Everyone knew that corporations still had too many people in them. But the dead wood had been cut from the workers – who was left to chop? Middle management. Companies wanted to be seen as lean and streamlined. They wanted to chop overheads that didn't pay – or didn't seem to pay. Middle management was the ideal layer to cut out as, supposedly, they didn't produce anything and thus were expendable. It was all about productivity.

If you use 100 people to make 100 items and then sack 50 of those people and still make your 100 items you must have increased productivity, profits and proficiency, mustn't you? Yes, in the short term. But it is blind management. It cannot see what happens within a very short time. You have lost the 50 people who did your selling, chasing orders, invoicing, research, investment, training, recruiting, new product development, debt collecting, and other essential tasks. It isn't a joke, that is what happened. Companies and corporations were literally so short-sighted that they ditched half their workforce and didn't realize until it was too late that they had effectively committed corporate suicide.

The companies were left with guilt-ridden senior management wondering how they had survived the chop and masses of slave labor who knew nothing about management or sales. Once the damage was done – and seen to be done – they needed to buy back in those same managers quickly. But those managers had wised up by now. They knew their value and knew the bargaining position they were in. They knew they had the expertise and knowledge the corporations so desperately needed. They had all the winning hands and all the chips. All the companies had was the table to play at and the beer.

THE RISE OF THE KNOWLEDGE WORKERS

And that's one of the routes we all took to the knowledge workers. In the last 20 years there has been a massive rise in knowledge workers for two reasons:

» the first reason we have already looked at – downsizing and its knock on effects; and
» the revolution in information technology.

Now, you don't want to be bored with a complete history of computers and IT, but it is interesting to look at some of the major developments and realize how quickly all this has happened. The rise of free agency runs hand in hand with the development of IT, the Internet and modern technological developments. And it ain't over yet. Even as this title goes into production someone somewhere is striving to make it all obsolete. And that's the way it should be.

Now, we're not going back to Babbage and his Analytical Machine of 1834. Instead, we can accept that it all really started with Vannevar Bush in 1930, who completed his Differential Analyzer for MIT. In 1937 Alan Turing published *On Computable Numbers*, where he proposed the hypothetical universal computer – later referred to as the Turing Machine in his honor. A year later Konrad Zuse built the first binary calculator – the Z1 – in Germany. Now you know where all those Zs so beloved of computer people come from.

In America Howard Aitken was working with IBM, completely independently, on a binary calculator. And a mere year after this Bell Laboratories built a Complex Number Calculator. The forties saw major technological developments, including the electronic tube, the first electromechanical program-controlled calculator, and the Mark 1 "electronic brain" at IBM. Obviously, the war brought swift and sudden breakthroughs, including the Colossus code-breaking machine.

In 1948 Norbert Wiener published *Cybernetics*, which described the idea of control by feedback and gave rise to the ideas that have influenced engineering, artificial intelligence, and social sciences ever since. Xerox machines became widely available and EDSAC was born – the first full scale electronic stored program computer at Cambridge University.

The fifties saw similar rapid developments, with IBM developing its first electronic computer.

By the early sixties, minicomputers were being produced by the Digital Equipment Corporation and MIT developed the first computer time-sharing system.

In 1976 the first Apple was designed and in 1977 the software company, Microsoft, was founded by Bill Gates, then aged just 16. And the rest, as they say, is history.

By the early eighties we had the first PC – and the first use of Usenet and the first bulletin boards – and by the mid-eighties Apple Macs were marketed, fax machines appeared, and the first computer virus was detected – at the University of Delaware.

We had the first inklings of the Internet in 1982, with Netnews distributing 500 messages per day to 100 sites in newsgroups. And by 1986 NSFnet opened the Internet access to all.

Only six years later there were one million Internet hosts, 10,000 news messages per day in over 1,000 newsgroups. And three years later in 1996 we had exceeded 10 million Internet hosts. The revolution was here. The mid-nineties saw the creation of search engines – Lycos and Yahoo, by Java and Netscape respectively.

Once the technology was in place it took no time at all for people to begin using it – and using it both to talk to each other and to trade. Once trading was going on it wasn't a quantum leap to start using it for work – the age of the free agent was upon us.

EMPLOYER LOYALTY AND ITS DEMISE

So what causes so many people – remember from Chapter 1 the figure of between 9 and 30 million people in the US alone who may be classified as free agents – to get up and walk away from a highly paid, highly protected job and branch out on their own? The answer may well be that they were initially forced to, and later wanted to, once they had been given a taste of freedom.

We are all primitive people in the sense that we haven't evolved much from early cave dwellers. There simply hasn't been enough time since we first used fire to evolve into anything new. Our responses are exactly the same as they were 10,000 years ago. We ain't budged a bit. When we are threatened we still have a fight or flight response. We still feel the need to be part of a tribe or community and we shall still defend our cave to the death.

So what's happened to our cave in the last 20 years? It has been threatened. First they gave us open plan caves. Then they took our desks away. Once you've altered the cave – the office – beyond all recognition, you've removed any employee loyalty. The thinking seems to go "if they think they can monkey around with my space then I'm outta here". And we left.

Add to this the recessions of the seventies and eighties when corporations thought absolutely nothing of laying off vast numbers of workers at the drop of a balance sheet and you can see why there isn't any loyalty left. The corporations started it with their first salvo of redundancies and hot desking. The staff have retaliated by becoming knowledge workers prepared to sell their services to the highest bidder. Who cares about "the company" any more? None of us are company men or women anymore because we were forced to rethink our position. And during that rethinking process we discovered the tools to fight back with – the Internet, computers, mobile phones. We might have had the desk pulled out from under us but we were prepared to re-install our desk elsewhere. For some of us that has been at home but for a lot of free agents they now carry their desk around with them – their own space.

THE END OF PSYCHOLOGICAL CONTRACTS

We have a different mind set to our fathers and mothers. We are more creative when it comes to employment. The money alone isn't the issue any more. Consider Anne Sweeney, who was offered the presidency of the Disney channel. She didn't ask herself about the value of the stock options or whether her take home pay would be sufficient. Instead she asked herself the one question "will this job make my heart sing?". Once she had decided it would, she accepted the offer. We all want our work to make our hearts sing. The difference between what the lowest employer offers and the highest isn't that great any more. Instead we seek different satisfactions. We want to learn more, expand our range of skills, be challenged. And we will go to the company which offers us these opportunities.

Only the most progressive, most innovative companies will recruit the best free agents. And we also seek a moral dimension too. Look what happened to Shell once its Nigerian links were publicized. Its recruitment campaign of graduates fell off drastically. We all want a company to reflect our own social and ethical concerns.

The free agents are free to work for those whom they best feel suit those social and ethical concerns. And they have the power to demand changes. The mind set is different and the free agents, in a lot of cases, have the clout to back up their demands. There has to be an end to the psychological contract because we are all now too clever to be sucked in any more.

THE MOVE TO SHORT-TERM CONTRACTS

Thomas Edison said "I have not failed. I've just found 10,000 ways that don't work." And we haven't failed when we change jobs frequently. We might just have found 10,000 jobs that didn't work – for us. If our working life is that much shorter now – knock off a lot for further education, university, postgrad courses and the such like, and knock off a lot for early retirement, etc. at the other end – then the bit in the middle where we actually do something is very short indeed. We simply don't have time to work for one company too long – or even long enough any more. We want to move in, make our kill, and move on. That's the way of the modern workers. Perhaps it is the advertising we have all been subjected to for so long that gives us such a short attention span or maybe it is all in the way films are cut in short, snappy sequences that make us so restless. It doesn't matter what the cause, the damage – or evolution – has occurred. We no longer even consider long-term contracts. Even six months now seems a shade on the long side. We have been used to so much, so quickly, that we need fresh stimulation at a frightening rate. Try any web site, if it doesn't load faster than you can blink then we're outta there, onto the next one, surfing faster than we can click.

Work has become more than a means of earning money. It now reflects our self-image. We ask our children what they will *be* when they are grown-ups – not what they will *do*. It is the same for us. We don't *do* programming or engineering, we *are* programmers or engineers. In a recent survey in the US nearly 85% of the populations said their work was an important part of their self-worth. Who is going to sign a long-term contract when our self-worth changes so often? We need our work to bolster our self-image, to enable us to feel good about ourselves. We turn to self-help, therapy, group support, training courses, online discussion groups – but not to our employer – when we need to grow and improve. We have become the equal of our employer and no longer see them as an authority figure. The employer has been demystified. The same is now happening to politicians. Who will sign a long-term contract when you don't trust the other side?

THE CHANGE IN ATTITUDES TO EMPLOYMENT

Once it was considered a requirement to hate your work. We all complained that it was "just a job." But there has been quite a revolution recently and work is now seen as not only necessary but as an essential part of human development and activity. Without work we grow stagnant and dull. More and more our work has to challenge us and stimulate us. Enormous resources are poured into training, motivating, and keeping staff. Once workers were seen as mere cannon fodder – bodies to man the machines. But we have a dimension no machine can possibly have – we are creative. Give us sufficient motivation and we will work long hours, work harder than ever before, and move mountains to get a job done.

Work is fun and enjoyable – it just takes a little shift in our thinking to acknowledge that. And employers who fail to make that shift lose valuable workers. We all want more than just a pay packet at the end of the week or month. We want responsibility, fresh challenges, and new directions. Where once we might have been happy to settle into a long-term career with gradual promotion and a decent pension at the end of it, we no longer find that fits. We are no longer persuaded by the money alone. The change in attitudes to employment has risen up from the bottom. Graduates set the pace now because they bring a new way of working into employment. They have camped out at rock festivals and know they can still function on a Monday morning. They refuse to wear ties and demand greater flexibility. And they have the clout to back up their demands. They are a forceful and dynamic new working phenomenon.

Any company that wants to stay ahead in the most fiercely competitive market ever has to take account of this new approach to work. We can't expect people to sit in dark and cramped offices all day and still produce their best work. We have to send them out into the coffee houses and Internet cafes to meet with other like-minded workers. The exchange of information is now so instant, so easily accessed that we can't use the outmoded working arrangements of the last century. There is a revolution happening and the smarter companies and corporations are moving swiftly with the tide to catch the best of this sea change.

LEARNING POINTS

» More mobile workforces.
» The framework of employer/employee.
» Standard Oil.
» Bill Gates.
» The industrial revolution.
» World Wars x 2.
» The shift to self-employment.
» The role of women in World War II.
» Employment landscapes.
» East vs West.
» Jobs for life.
» Downsizing.
» Buying back in knowledge.
» The revolution in IT.
» History of IT employer/employee loyalty.
» Taking away the desks.
» Anne Sweeney.
» Ethical concerns.
» Short-term contracts.
» Self-worth.
» The fun of work.

The E-Dimension

Free agents can capitalize greatly on the new developments within the Internet. How will they rise to these new challenges? How can corporations and companies make best use of the Internet? This chapter deals with these issues.

» Implications of the Internet and IT
» Liberating people from their offices
» Free agents working for clients anywhere in the world
» The boost to free agency
» Free agent interview – case study

"It is the right of every independent agent to use his or her time to make decisions, not stuff, to be productive, not busy, and to leverage every moment to make a difference, not just dollars."

Seth Godin, online marketing maverick based in Dobbs Ferry,
New York http://ideavirus.com author of e-book
The Big Red Fez: How to Make Any Web Site Better

IMPLICATIONS OF THE INTERNET AND IT

As we saw in the last chapter the history of computers, IT, and the Internet has been one of a swift and meteoric rise to fame and success. The last five years have seen such changes that none of us has really had time to work out all the implications yet. But what we do see is that those who are capable of grabbing this new technology can steal a march on their competitors, be they other free agents or other corporations seeking independent professionals.

Thus the implication of the Internet and IT is that these are tools to be seized and used to their utmost capabilities. In the old days a designer might well have been recruited using an ad along the following lines.

Company X currently has the following positions open:

Designer

Job Description: Design manufacturing test stations, fixturing, and tools for the aid in yield improvement of laser diode manufacturing. Create and maintain assembly details with BOMs from Solidworks models. Keep and maintain updated drawings per engineering change notices. Work directly with designers and engineers on tooling, fixtures, new products, and company support.

Minimum Requirements: Candidate should have strong background in manufacturing design. Familiar with automation techniques and technology. Applicants should have 2-3 years' CAD experience (Solidworks preferred). Individual must be trained in ANSI Y14.5M drafting standards. Familiarity with standard geometric tolerancing a plus. Must be familiar with Microsoft Office.

Now consider Bruce Mau, who runs a pretty big prestigious design studio – the BMD. When he wanted to recruit new staff he put out a quiz with some 40 questions including such as "Who made a film consisting of nothing but the color blue?" Derek Jarman of course.

Bruce headed the ad "Avoid fields. Jump fences." Result: he lured some of the best, most talented top designers to come and work for him – or *with* him as he describes his working relationship with his staff.

The Internet has given us all the tools we need to be independent, creative, and multifunctional. The old methods of working are now so outmoded as to be positively dinosaur-like – extinct. Trouble is, a lot of companies haven't yet entirely wised up to this new development. We aren't going back. The Internet is here to stay now. Pandora's box has been opened and we can't close it again – even if we wanted to.

LIBERATING PEOPLE FROM THEIR OFFICES

It's all getting smaller. The laptop enables us to work from the bottom of the garden. Email and voice mail means we no longer have to be physically anywhere anymore. We have been liberated from our office. First they took our desks away and then we took ourselves away. We now have the facilities to carry our office around in a briefcase – or any other sort of case we choose. If we keep our options open and our thinking clear and lateral, we don't need the huge resources a corporation offers. In fact we can work more effectively if we free ourselves of all the stuff big companies have to have. A classic example of this is the US space program. They needed a pen that would write in space. Ink uses gravity and there ain't none out there in the big blue. So they spent $25mn on developing a pen that would work. Great. The Russians had the same problem. Their solution? Pencils.

You don't need a lot to do a lot. You need to keep in sight your endgame, not the vehicle making the journey. This is where free agents can score so highly. Free agents are interested in getting the job done and getting out again. They don't seek the status of promotion or fancy job titles or even fancy offices. They are just as happy to work in a shed in the backyard as in some highfalutin penthouse suite in downtown Smogsville.

FREE AGENTS WORKING FOR CLIENTS ANYWHERE IN THE WORLD

And once free agents have made the move to their shed or kitchen or wherever they fancy they are also free to work for anyone anywhere in the world. The Internet when used as an advertising board is fantastic for liberating free agents from the constraints of commuting or working only for local employers. OK, there are a lot of jobs which can only be done on site. But there are an awful lot more which don't require personal attendance. Once companies can be got over the "come in for a meeting" stuff free agents can easily work from home or wherever takes their fancy – just so long as the job gets done and the company is happy with the end result.

THE BOOST TO FREE AGENCY

Free agents don't even have to rely on postal services anymore. Large volumes of work can be dispatched and delivered via email, telephone conferencing has taken the place of the face-to-face meeting and computer shall speak directly unto computer. Of course, people still need the interaction of personal contact, which is why there is a growing implementation of guilds in the US. These are loose federations of like-minded souls and like-skilled people getting together to discuss their work and their problems. These aren't unions in the old fashioned sense but in time they too will have some clout, as malpractice by employers gets discussed and routed out.

The tremendous rise in free agency – especially in the US – has mainly come about because of the new dimension of e-commerce. As more and more of us become familiar with the new technology and conversant with it, it becomes easier to conduct more and more business over the net.

BEST PRACTICE
Carol A. Hughes Tucker

Objective: To participate in creating an environment that affirms the contributions of each individual and emphasizes knowledge sharing and creation as the source of employee value to the organization and the organization's value to the customer and other stakeholders.

Professional Profile: Extensive background in positions requiring a high degree of accuracy, investigation, and deadline awareness with a focus on meeting and exceeding customer expectations. Experienced project manager. Works well with individuals from diversified backgrounds and at all levels of management. Effective communicator co-ordinating with multiple departments. Comprehensive industry knowledge. Excellent analytical and investigative skills. Proven track record in selecting and approving loans; knowledgeable regarding lending laws as well as compliance and regulatory issues.

Summary of Qualifications:

» Unique combination of lending experience, both consumer and commercial, coupled with a solid working familiarity with operational functions and issues.
» Strong communication skills – the ability to communicate openly, assertively, and effectively, and to encourage both subordinates and peers to do the same, achieving mutual understandings.
» The ability to identify, analyze, and solve problems, challenging conventional practices; excelling in futuristic and systematic thinking; always maintaining a high level of curiosity and displaying strong powers of observation; able to adapt quickly to new situations.
» A proven commitment to team-building efforts that is demonstrated by a personal and professional commitment to continuous improvement and the effective development of individual, team, and organizational goals.

FREE AGENT INTERVIEW – CASE STUDY

Debbie Weil, president of WordBiz.com and a very good example not only of being a free agent but of doing it properly and successfully, was happy to be interviewed to explain her thinking and development.

Was the Internet much help in becoming a free agent?

The Internet and the Web made it possible. Without the Internet and the Web as communications and research tools, I could not function as a free agent.

Did you encounter opposition from family/friends?

Not opposition – but polite skepticism. As in, "Oh, that's interesting. You're working out of a home office? So when are you going to get a job?" The message was: if you don't have a "real job," then it's not "real work."

Have you encountered problems with corporations/companies as a free agent?

Interestingly, no. People rarely ask me how many folks work for my company (currently, it's one – me – although I do have a part-time assistant). And they don't seem to care. People would prefer to work with the "principal" anyway, rather than a junior subordinate.

Has the tax position been a problem?

No, not so far. This is my first year as an incorporated entity. My expenses will be high so I don't expect to pay much tax.

Are you happier?

Absolutely and remarkably so. In fact, it surprises me. Since I made up my mind to strike out as a free agent (in my case, a "micro corporation") not quite a year ago, I have rarely had second thoughts. A fancy job title (VP of marketing) and stock options no longer have appeal. I will admit that I was utterly seduced by job/title/salary/options during the dot com boom. But desire for that kind of "legitimacy" has completely faded away. Plus I do not miss my corporate cubicle. (I was a marketing manager for a big Internet company from 1998–2000.) I was dying there – my soul was shriveling up. Although I don't think I realized it at the time.

Would you advise anyone else to become a free agent?

Sure. If they're willing to work harder than ever, to put themselves on the line, to try new things (speaking engagements, for example) – and if they can tolerate not getting a steady pay check.

What was the biggest challenge you've yet encountered?

"Closing the sale" with potential clients; negotiating contracts; discussing hourly and project rates – in a word, money. Unless your professional background is in sales, this is not a skill that you've necessarily developed in the corporate workplace.

What drawbacks do you see to being a free agent?

The only drawback is lack of a steady pay check.

Do you have a brief resume?

Please see my Web site at http://www.wordbiz.com/resume.html

Debbie Weil is President of WordBiz.com, Inc., a Washington DC-based strategy and copywriting firm specializing in B2B (business to business) email marketing, e-newsletters and Web content. She specializes in B2B online marketing, email and content strategy.

WordBiz has a bottom-line, sales-oriented focus. Whether it's an email message or compelling Web content, the objective is to turn "clicks" (aka visitors) into customers.

She is currently a regular columnist for ClickZ.com on B2B email marketing and has written about Internet business and technology issues for such publications as Internet.com's *WebDeveloper* and InternetWorld.com's *WebWeek*.

In 1995, she co-founded DC Web Women, now widely recognized as a leading online community, and resource for women in new media.

Debbie consults, speaks and writes on the topics of email marketing, effective messaging, and Web strategy.

KEY LEARNING POINTS

» IT and the Internet.
» Liberating people from their offices.
» Free agents working for clients anywhere in the world.
» Boosting free agency.
» Free agent interview – Debbie Weil – president of WordBiz.com.

The Global Dimension

As the world seems to shrink, free agents can consider the entire global economy their oyster bed. This chapter looks at how a global economy affects being a free agent and how global organizations can benefit from free agents.

» The implications of globalization
» The issues raised
» The one-person global business
» The global Website designer

"Free agents are swelling the ranks of the self employed. Half of small business owners are independent contractors."
Current Population Survey, US Department of Labor

THE IMPLICATIONS OF GLOBALIZATION

Every country has always had its own free agents. As industry has spread so have the demand for and needs of the free agents. We all now speak a universal language – MS-DOS – and can communicate with anyone anywhere in the world at pretty well any time. Borders are now meaningless as far as trade is concerned. They might still have a political or military agenda but to us IT workers and programmers and designers they have all but disappeared. If we don't have to physically move around the planet we have all become international citizens of the world.

And we all speak the same language – apart from MS-DOS of course – English. This might be very different – as someone once said the British and the Americans are one nation divided by a single language – but we can make ourselves understood. In a way we have all become radical extremists. We aren't constrained by barriers of trade or taxation or international law. The Internet has quickly become the outlaw's highway to freedom. We move around freely, often not knowing who we are communicating with or where they are from or even, at times, what gender they might be. And none of it matters. The free agency of the twenty-first century is designed to globalize us all by the very fact that it is so impossible to police. Who governs the ungovernable? When there are no rules, who will regulate us? We will do it ourselves. Increasingly those using the Internet are setting up their own rules and regulations. Spamming is outlawed not by some bureaucracy but by the unsubscribed members of the superhighway.

THE ISSUES RAISED

By the very fact of its lack of regulation the Internet has also become a vast dumping ground for nonsense and junk. It is also used by illegal organizations to promote their own particular agenda. With the prospect of international and global freedom we have to also accept that the loonies and cranks are out there as well. And the unscrupulous of course. There is money to be made out of the naïve, the unwary, the innocent, and the inexperienced – and there are enough sharks swimming in the ether to take advantage of them all. Free agents have to be on their guard against being used by those who have no morals and no scruples. Free agents will also have to fend off attack from those who seek to regulate the unregulatable.

We are like children who have been given the key to Pandora's box and how we use the unquenchable supply of information available will be up to us. If we use it responsibly and well we will prosper and succeed. If we are foolish and immature we will flounder under the weight of it all and sink into the morass of too much, too easy, and too readily available.

The Internet can be a huge tool for good or a vast repository of the banal and the dangerous. Consider for a moment that around 80% of all Internet usage is for pornography – scary that isn't it? But it's a fact. We can enter that Babylon or we can choose to use the Internet to further ourselves mentally, spiritually, and karmically. What we post will return to haunt us.

But the Internet doesn't solve all our logistical problems. We still have to physically move around and this poses a whole new raft of issues. Consider for a moment that you run a successful computer design and development company. You desperately need designers and engineers and programmers. The free agents in your own country are skilled, experienced, and very expensive. Do you continue to use them or go down the route of importing cheaper free agents from Mexico or India? Your accounts people will tell you the budget requirements and your managers will outline their needs and demands. Who do you listen to? Is it OK to use cheaper labor from another country? What do you tell yourself? That it's OK as they will still be earning more than they would in their own country so you are doing them a favor?

The British army encountered similar problems when they recruited Gurkhas. When a Gurkha soldier retires after long and active service in the British army what should he receive in the way of a pension? A full whack same as a retiring British soldier? Or a reduced amount but still pretty hefty by Nepalese standards? Whatever you do, you set up tensions and problems. Pay the Gurkhas a full pension and they have a much higher income than their Nepalese contemporaries which gives them undue power and influence when they return home. Pay them less and they still have more but feel hard done by and resentful.

American computer companies have been recruiting Indian software engineers for the past few years. This has benefitted both sides of the equation. But not any longer. Things are going desperately wrong. Thousands of Indian software engineers are being forced to return home because the economic slowdown in the US has forced businesses to cut back. Reports from Bombay and Bangalore have suggested that around 10,000 techies have already been forced to return home and as many as another 50,000 are expected to follow them by the end of this year (2001).

These techies are highly valued in the US for their skills and experience. They, however, have to apply for visas and face the problems of immigration. Around half of the H1B visas issued to software professionals by the US authorities went to Indians.

But the changing economic climate has forced companies to lay off staff and to stop recruiting. The worst hit have been the Indian IT workers who were hired out to American companies through body shops who have refused to pay their air fares home. A lot of Indian engineers are opting not to return home but to hang onto their visas in the hope that they will find another job or that the economic situation will take an upturn.

Those that have returned home may be more hopeful, as Japan is planning to hire up to 10,000 software engineers from India to meet their acute shortage of qualified IT workers. It is a global village indeed. There are problems with Indian workers going to Japan – the language problem, the differing views that the two countries hold on the nuclear issue – but a major Japanese firm, – Pasona, – has already set up a recruitment center in India and is planning an education center alongside to help overcome the cultural and language difficulties.

THE ONE-PERSON GLOBAL BUSINESS

It is now perfectly feasible to run a one-person global business. And there are quite a few out there. Problem is, you don't know which ones they are. For instance, how many people run the following company?

We are an online content and Internet marketing firm that focuses on customer acquisition and retention through permission email marketing, e-newsletters, and Web content.

We put a premium on great copy and on content that drives revenues. (And yes, we provide the "words," with killer copywriting services.)

Our approach is bottom-line and sales driven whether we are developing compelling, relevant content for your monthly e-newsletter, negotiating rental lists for your acquisition campaign, or identifying just the right email vendor to deliver your messages.

We have a B2B (business-to-business) focus because, frankly, it's more interesting than selling sweaters online. Whether you're immersed in email marketing and looking for better results – or just starting out – we can help.

We can work with you for a day on a strategic level to get you up to speed on the latest in permission email marketing tactics and e-newsletters. As part of that, we make initial recommendations for how your company can turn "clicks" (aka visitors) into customers.

Or we can do it for you. We can develop and maintain an e-newsletter that will bring your target audience (your in-house email list) back to your site again and again – resulting in sales down the road.

If your goal is to acquire email addresses, we can design an email acquisition campaign that will drive visitors from your email message – or sponsorship text ad – to register on your site.

Our goal is to leverage the speed, cost-efficiency, and effectiveness of email so that it becomes a key piece of an integrated – on- and off-line – marketing strategy.

Feel free to call us directly if you'd like to know more about how we can help you.

What's your greatest need? To lower the cost of customer acquisition? To shorten your sales cycle? To generate more qualified leads? Tell us and we'll work with you to translate your business objective into compelling content on your site and in your e-newsletters.

See also: global wordbiz | wireless wordbiz

Call us or email us for more details on how we can help you.

Partial client list

Our client list includes: Liquidation.com; LeapFrog Solutions; Hotel Net Marketing; eGrail; and Beyond Words Marketing Communications.

Also: Discovery Online International; Blackboard, Inc.; Cross-Media Networks; AtYourOffice.Com; America Online; and the Newspaper Association of America.

Answer: one.

We looked at WordBiz.com in the last section. It is possible for any one person to launch and run a company that looks like a truly global and fully staffed business by effective presentation and professionalism.

THE GLOBAL WEBSITE DESIGNER

I know of one Website designer who also happens to be a surfer. He runs his business from various beaches in Spain and Portugal from his Mercedes camper van. All he needs is his laptop, his mobile phone hooked up via a satellite connection and a fully charged battery pack. No one knows that he is sitting in his shorts sipping ice cold beer waiting for the next big wave. He has worked for some pretty big companies, including ones in the US, Russia, Germany, Sweden, the UK, France and a new lead will be taking him into China soon. Not physically of course. He is mobile, free, creative, and extremely employable. He doesn't own a tie let alone wear one. He enjoys his life, works hard when he needs to, and is truly a free agent. He is a free agent because he fulfils all the requirements of free agency:

» he is independent;
» he picks when and where he will work;
» he sells his knowledge rather than a product;
» he works on a set project and then moves on; and
» he decides who he will work for and negotiates his own contracts.

But he is a one-person company. What about the big ones? Well here's a highly successful global free agency.

BEST PRACTICE BOX

Eutech Cybernetics, founded in 1990, is a software development company, specializing in innovative software solutions for Intelligent Buildings, Facilities Management, and Networked Healthcare Organisations. Eutech Cybernetics has over 70 International Customers today.

Eutech Cybernetics is a Singapore – based company having overseas operations in California and Pittsburgh (USA), Chennai (India), Kuala Lumpur (Malaysia) and Colombo (Sri Lanka).

Eutech has pursued strategic relationships, alliances, and joint ventures to create technology excellence centers and support the dynamic business of its customers. Eutech provides strong local support for implementing its solutions through a growing partner network.

The State of the Art

Free agency is constantly evolving. So what news is breaking even as we read that affects this topic?

» Key issues today
» Current debate
» Negotiating with individuals on a project by project basis
» Looking to the future
» The shift from salaries to performance-based remuneration
» Flexible working arrangements
» Case study
» The change in the role of the manager

"People are starting home businesses at a rate of 2 million per year."

American Demographics Magazine

KEY ISSUES TODAY

I think we've pretty well covered in earlier parts what constitutes a free agent and how the corporations work with them. Free agents are free to sell their services. The corporations are free to hire them. In an ideal world all would progress smoothly and happily. But wake up and smell the coffee. It ain't an ideal world. Just when we are getting it together and forging a successful working relationship there are the party poopers who seek to interfere. Yes, the tax offices in whatever nation state you wind up working in. There are quite a lot of forward-thinking governments – especially in Europe – who can see that this issue is an emerging one and it might be best to sit on the sidelines for a while and see which way the wind will blow. The progressives realize that this new working relationship can benefit both sides – and that means an upturn in trade. They figure it might be better to lay off now and collect taxes from increased trade later than to try and kill the golden goose before it's even started cackling. In some less progressive nation states the goose is being strangled before it's even been allowed to be born.

If the free agents are happy with the situation... Well, no one is strong-arming them into being happier, more motivated, more challenged, more creative, and a better use being made of their time. And no one is forcing the corporations to turn out their full-time workers. Then who really is so short-sighted as to interfere? Yes, you got it. Let's look at one case in particular. Granted it's a big one but important nonetheless. This might not affect all the free agents or all the corporations, but it's best to know what Goliath is using in the way of defenses these days before loading our sling.

CURRENT DEBATE

After Microsoft got into hot water with the IRS in the late eighties, the company requested that most of its free agents sign up with an employment agency so Microsoft could hire them back. But before they were allowed to return Microsoft insisted that they sign a contract saying that they were temporary workers and not full-time employees. Normally, if people sign a contract saying that they know they're not going to get any benefits, that settles the matter once and for all. But the courts later ruled that the temporary workers had signed an invalid contract. The court's ruling was that no matter what waiver you sign, your job is what it appears to be – if you look like a full-time employee then that's what you are. If it looks like a duck and walks like a duck and quacks, then it's no use the duck insisting it's a swan.

Once the courts had established that the contracts were invalid they had to determine which of the employees had the right to sue – and who their true employer was. Was it Microsoft or the employment agency? According to the current legislation the worker could be working under an employment agency contract and still be an employee of the company.

To get a definitive ruling, the courts, with the assistance of the IRS, who have the right to be included in any such rulings, have developed a benchmark that takes many different standards into account – up to 20 by some estimates. The courts are supposed to apply this benchmark or standards to determine the correct relationship between employee and employer. According to this test, there could be more than 10,000 temporary workers who were actually full-time employees and who could therefore be eligible to sue somebody.

But what are the temporary workers supposed to sue for? Even though the contracts described their status incorrectly, they were not necessarily entitled to receive benefits – with one exception: Microsoft's employee stock-purchase plan (ESPP). That plan allows an employee to purchase Microsoft stock at a 15% discount on the lowest price that the stock had reached in the six-month period prior to that employee's making the purchase. In order for Microsoft to receive the kind of lucrative tax breaks that make it possible to offer an ESPP, the plan requires the company to allow any full-time employee to participate – whether or not they are entitled by dint of their supposedly being an employment agency worker. So, once the courts determined that temporary workers were, in fact, ipso facto employees these temporary workers became eligible to participate, retroactively, in the ESPP.

So how much stock might the temporary workers have bought had they known that they were eligible to buy it? Well, one possible way of finding out is to look at how much buying and selling took place amongst other employees. Since the early nineties nearly 80% of all full-time Microsoft employees have purchased stock through the ESPP at any given time. So the upshot of it all is that Microsoft could be liable for many millions of dollars.

So what caused Microsoft to carry on employing such large numbers of free agents even after the late eighties ruling? There doesn't seem to be any one single answer. They weren't saving that much money – at least not enough to warrant taking on the courts and the IRS. Employing what has become termed ''permatemps'' – temporary workers who stay so long they might just as well be permanent workers – might be a hedge against bad times when the company, any company, might be forced to lay off large numbers of staff with all the attendant costs.

It could be a hedge against bad publicity. In a recession you have to lay off lots of full-time staff, which attracts the media. But if all your workers are temps or free agents then you just say their contracts have expired and you attract no media attention at all. It's a fact of life but one which large corporations might well be happy to milk.

There are some that say the culture of Microsoft itself inspires the sort of attitude where free agents are given extra status – if you come from an entrepreneurial background you might not want to get bogged down with running a ''proper'' company with an ever-growing mass of dependent full-time employees. Better to let the free agents carry on the job you started.

On the other hand entirely, it might be a completely unplanned accident. The courts that have been handling the lawsuit say that there has been no deliberate or malicious intent on the part of Microsoft. Microsoft made a series of individual decisions about whom to hire full-time and whom to hire through an agency; somewhere along the way, those decisions led to the creation of a class of permatemp workers. It may well have just been poor management practice that spiraled out of control.

NEGOTIATING WITH INDIVIDUALS ON A PROJECT BY PROJECT BASIS

When you have to negotiate with free agents on a project by project basis it doesn't half sharpen up your thinking. Woolly managers went away with the ice age. Today we need managers who can clearly identify what needs doing and then collect the best resources, including people to get that job done. When a manager has to justify their actions on a project by project basis it helps clarify the endgame – what the project is all about. It helps define the end of a job and the beginning of the next. They have to negotiate the project with the free agent. They need to know themselves a time scale, a rough cost, and a benchmark for completion or satisfactory conclusion.

LOOKING TO THE FUTURE

So what does the future hold? Well, a lot of uncertainty – that's certain. Even as this title is being prepared, things are changing. In the UK a landmark ruling by the European Court of Justice (June 26, 2001) will mean that UK employers are going to have to change their 13 week qualification period for paid holidays. The Court ruled that the UK government had broken employment law by denying those with less than 13 weeks, continuous employment the right to annual paid leave. This new ruling will have wide ramifications for the free agency business and freelance and contract workers in certain industries such as supply teaching, the media, and employment agencies, where employment contracts tend to be of short duration.

The case was brought by a broadcasting union – BECTU – and it marks a new development in employment law as it is the first time an individual union has taken the UK government to the European court.

So what does it mean for free agents? Possibly that if a free agent is working for any one single employer for longer than 13 weeks they may well be entitled to holiday pay. But this could mean they are classified by the Inland Revenue as full-time employees and thus lead to an increase in their tax liability by markedly reducing their claimable expenses.

THE SHIFT FROM SALARIES TO PERFORMANCE-BASED REMUNERATION

It is a fact that over the last 20 years employers have grown very canny. No longer are they prepared to tolerate dead wood – employees who are there just for the pay check at the end of the month. Instead employers want lean and mean workforces who are paid by result. But employees increasingly also want to be paid by result. There is no point busting a gut just to collect the same money as the bozo at the next desk who coasts. "Do more, get more" is the motto of every hard-working free agent.

This system works well for both sides when the workforce is lean and motivated and the employers keen to get a job done that can be measured by results. But there still have to be nurses and teachers, firefighters and sewerage workers. It gets hard to pay by result when the results are difficult to quantify. A lot of employers will attempt to quantify results by imposing some form of benchmark testing but, as in the above instance, where we are dealing with an issue such as nursing, it really does get very hard indeed. How do we pay? Number of patients who make a good recovery with deductions for any dead ones? Probably not. Employers are then led to false benchmarking such as good timekeeping, attitude, presentation, that sort of thing. And then we are into another ball game altogether. Anyone can fake the timekeeping and attitude stuff and still be lousy at their job and not be working to their utmost. Others may fall down on such tests but be simply brilliant at their job. How do you judge when the situation can't be judged?

And for a lot of operatives such as computer programmers the same sort of non-ideal situation occurs. How can you pay someone by result when they are engaged in research? Obviously a lot of research ends in blind alleys. What do you do then? Refuse to pay the free agent because their research didn't lead to a profitable product?

Paying by result can succeed if the work is:

» quantifiable;
» has an "end product";
» is easily monitored; or
» can be benchmarked.

And the opposite is obviously true. Paying by result is difficult if the work is:

» not quantifiable;
» has no end product;
» is difficult to monitor; or
» can't be benchmarked.

More and more free agents are what is known as "information nego-tiators" – they have certain information which an employer needs. The free agent sells that information to the employer in exchange for money. Their information is often utilized as a talent or skill – i.e. that information has to be put to a useful function – but the negotiation is still the same; information in exchange for money. This is fairly easy to pay for by result – if the employer doesn't end up with the information, they don't pay – simple really.

Free agents who have a talent or skill to offer end up being paid easily by result as it is a simple equation – so many widgets screwed onto so many whatnots per hour.

So we have looked at three possible areas of paying by result:

» information negotiators;
» skilled workers; and
» workers who for one reason or another will find it harder to be paid by result.

It is this last category who will remain longest as full-time paid employees, purely because their work is so difficult to quantify. And one of the tests for anyone thinking of going solo as a free agent is for them to ask themselves "Is my work easily quantifiable?." If it isn't they may need to rethink their strategy.

FLEXIBLE WORKING ARRANGEMENTS

I don't know about anyone else but I do my best work at around 2 a.m. Now, if I worked for a corporation instead of being a free agent I would only ever give them my worst, my 9 to 5 shot. Now I can give my customers – be they companies, corporations, e-businesses, whatever – my best time. I can do my best work at the time it suits me.

The whole point of free agency is that the boundaries between work and home get blurred. I might be sitting at supper with my family when an email sounds in and I quickly respond – "Yes, I can do this job later, hold tight and I'll get back to you" – and then return to discussing what the kids did at school today. I no longer have a specific "work time" and then a "home time." I work when the mood takes me and socialize when I need to. I do have clear boundaries in that I don't work weekends.

CASE STUDY

Consider the case of Tom Hawks. Tom worked for several leading advertising agencies both in the UK and later in the US. He is a copywriter – he writes the text that accompanies the ads. He clocked on, did his 9 to 5, wore a suit and a tie, was a good company man, collected his wage at the need of the month, and used the company facilities. They, in turn, gave him a decent salary, gave him a car, gave him a pension. What they didn't give him was motivation, inspiration, and pleasure. Let Tom tell it:

"I was bored out of my skull. I spent too much time beating off the gossips, the time wasters, people playing petty politics. I didn't seem to get enough time actually working on stuff I wanted to. I also had to spend a lot of time going to meetings about things which could have been settled with a phone call. I was stagnating, rotting even. But I had a young family to support and couldn't see that walking out was the answer.

"I started to suffer badly from stress and my hair was falling out. I went to an acupuncturist as my doctor couldn't do anything. He said that if I didn't quit doing what I was doing other things might start to go wrong soon as well. My energy was dead, lifeless, sluggish. When your health starts to suffer you have to make a move. I walked.

"The first few months were tough. I tried writing to all the agencies I had worked for but they seemed terribly old fashioned and wouldn't allow me to work from home. Then I discovered lots of other companies on the Internet – and not just advertising ones – which wanted stuff written for them. They seemed refreshingly new and able to handle the fact that I didn't want to buy into their company stuff. I just wanted to do the work and leave the rest alone. I now wear jeans. Work out of a back room in our house in New Mexico. Never travel to company offices and feel good about what I do. And I'm earning a lot more than I was. No, the hair didn't grow back but that's cool, it reminds me of how bad it was. I'm a free agent now, and free to live better and, I hope, longer.''

If free agency is to carry on working well and grow, corporations have to accept that flexible working arrangements make sense. Yes, the job has to be done. But we are all grown-ups here and the job will be done if we are allowed to have the freedom to work at our own pace – which in most cases is faster than full-time employees, as we are more motivated: more jobs done, more money for us. We don't need anyone breathing down our necks, looking over our shoulders, or chasing our tails. This has led to a revolution in what the role of the manager really is.

THE CHANGE IN THE ROLE OF THE MANAGER

Your in-line manager used to be your boss. Not any more. We don't have bosses now. A boss was someone who told you what to do, made sure you did it and then picked holes in the way you did it. Today the manager has to be a motivator, a people person capable of talking our language, able to inspire and supervise while staying out of the way. Modern managers aren't bosses, they're facilitators. Their job is to provide you with the best resources for you to make your job happen – and happen well. They are there to provide support and operational back-up. They should be a central meeting point of information and ideas and a link between you and the end-user of the products of your skills and talents. The manager nowadays isn't an overseer but a co-ordinator. They need to move with the times and realize that workers today need a helping hand, not one with a whip in it. The manager's job is to get the best out of people without getting in the way. Bruce Mau of the BMD design company – see Chapter 3 – has several homilies for his staff – and he is not only their manager but top boss as well. And if he can do it other managers can as well. He says to his fellow workers:

» **don't clean your desk** – you might find something in the morning that you couldn't see last night;
» **stay up late occasionally** – you make breakthroughs when you have pushed yourself too hard, too far and are too tired. Strange things happen when you are separated from the rest of the world;
» **drift** – allow yourself to wander aimlessly;
» **lack judgement** – allow yourself to make mistakes occasionally and benefit from the lessons they teach you; and
» **ask dumb questions** – your growth gets fuelled by innocence and desire.

And that is inspirational management. Bruce is motivating, supporting, encouraging, inspiring, co-ordinating, stimulating, and inspiring his staff. He ain't bossing no one. And he is getting the very best people to work with him because he has learnt the simple truth of management in the new economy – treat 'em like grown ups and they'll not let you down. Treat 'em like kids and they'll f**k up big time.

KEY LEARNING POINTS

» Key issues today.
» The tax debate.
» Permatemps.
» Microsoft and the IRS ruling.
» Looking to the future.
» The shift from salaries to performance-based remuneration.
» Paying by results.
» Information negotiators.
» Flexible working arrangements.
» The change in the role of the manager.
» Bruce Mau's advice to his workers.

In Practice: Free Agent Success Stories

So how do we go about being free agents or making best use of free agents? This chapter looks at two success stories as well as some drawbacks.

- » Case study of an independent professional
- » On becoming a free agent

"Predictions are that as technology, our society, culture, and workplaces change more and more in these ways over the next few years – each worker will become responsible for his/her own career."

Diana Fell Votech Education

CASE STUDY OF AN INDEPENDENT PROFESSIONAL

Arnie McKinnis

To be completely honest, I fell into the world of independent work. It wasn't a planned event. I hadn't been looking for the right opportunity to "jump ship." I became an independent worker through necessity. In the summer of 1994 I was the Director of Product Marketing for a network management company in New Jersey, then I was laid off. At that point I had a decision to make: remain in the Northeast United States and secure other employment or move and make a plan. I chose to move to familiar territory, my hometown of Oklahoma City, Oklahoma.

The initial plan was to "network" through friends and family, find a marketing position with a technology company in Oklahoma City, and continue my career. That proved a very difficult task. Dejected, I called an old friend to "vent" about my current situation. During the conversation, he mentioned an idle project that needed some dedicated attention. So on August 11, 1994, I was on a plane bound for Los Angeles to begin work on my first project. Little did I know, it would take me on a five-year journey through the peaks and valleys of being an independent worker.

This project, leading a team to define the "Service Delivery Model for Desktop Management and Outsourcing Services," was a raging success. It established me as an expert within the company (a Fortune 500 Professional Services Firm) and helped create credibility beyond the small group in Los Angeles. As my reputation grew within the company the projects began queuing up. The more I charged for my time, the more in demand I became. I was riding a wave that appeared to have no end in sight.

But I was naïve; I spent the majority of time networking and building business with this one client, not understanding that as an independent, it is important to create the widest circle of influence possible. I broke the first rule of business, never have to depend solely on one customer for 100% of your revenue. As a result, the company (my only client) decided to cut costs by eliminating all contractor positions. I was offered employment, but turned it down, thinking I could leverage my experience and contacts in the marketplace. I spent the next year in a vicious cycle of "Do Work/Find Work" and seeing myself first depleting my savings, then getting into debt. I had gone from making $6,000+ per week, to barely making my mortgage payments and eventually declaring bankruptcy. It was truly a dark time.

In the end, the only decision left was to "re-join" the ranks in Corporate America. After finding a job, it took approximately 12 months for me to "recover" mentally from the feelings of failure and another six months to determine a new course of action. Currently, I'm working as a mid-level manager in a Fortune 500 company. Three months ago, I began writing a book about marketing, selling, and delivering services, something I've done my whole career. I came to realize that being independent is a state of mind, not your tax status. So now I view myself as an internal consultant waiting for the opportunity to go independent again. But this time, I enter it with my eyes wide open and ready for the challenges ahead.

What advice would I give to either aspiring or current independent workers?

1 Cash flow is king – always have more money coming in than is going out. Sound business advice, but it takes discipline to break the pay check mentality.
2 Find a way to soften the financial "peaks and valleys" – balance your workload between business development and service delivery.
3 Be serious and treat it as a business – it's easy to take the independent life for granted, but you are in business to stay in business. Always take the long view.
4 Create a business base close to home – during lean times, it's nice not to have the expense of travel, but have the ability to keep cash flowing in.
5 Don't rely on one customer – if you need any encouragement, read my story above. You can have one BIG customer, but leverage the risk over several customers.

6 Charge twice as much as you think you should – this one is tough. Value your work, your specialty, your talent. It's always easier to lower your billing rate than it is to raise it.

7 Charge by the project/job, not by the hour – the world values efficiency.

8 If possible, keep all or part of the intellectual rights of your creations – some independents have used this little trick to create very lucrative residual incomes.

9 Stay active – through writing articles, speaking engagements, discussion boards on the Internet – anything that will help you stay noticed and help build credibility.

10 Choose who you work with (not for) – you went independent to have independence – never work for someone that doesn't value your work.

ON BECOMING A FREE AGENT

Kiki Ross, Ki2Net Intranet Solutions, London, UK

Introduction

It is exactly a year to this day that I have been working as a free agent. I reflect on the last 12 months with a mix of wonder and joy. I have learned, laughed, lived, and ultimately empowered myself this year. I recognize that I am beginning to satisfy the deep yearning for self-reliance, both personal and professional, and to savor this sense of freedom, which allows me to make conscious choices about how I spend each day. All along my path, I have known that it is my life's mission to be able to give myself this gift.

In order to explain more fully, I have detailed below the reasons I decided to become a free agent, the highlights, problems, benefits, and drawbacks. The mentoring and support I have received from family and friends as well as setting my own success factors have all had a crucial role.

What led me into it?

» A deep yearning to work for myself.
» A push from someone I respected who believed in me.

» The ability to minimize professional and financial risk.
» A commitment to be true to my mother's belief in me.

The problems I encountered

Confidence! This one word is behind every obstacle I continue to overcome each day. Even now, my stomach churns when I have to make cold calls! However, the feeling when I make the quota of calls, however successful, is quite exhilarating!

The support I have received from family and friends

A mentor: I have had an excellent mentor throughout this last year. She is an executive level marketing guru and she has always been there to give me the hard truth, and to know when I needed support and encouragement. An added bonus: she is also someone I can laugh with!

Financial backing – my father loaned me the finances to start up. He demonstrated he has faith in me and he will certainly be my first repayment check!

Intangible support from sisters, brothers, and their respective partners, who happily hand out tips on sales technique, accounting, and administration, and who tease you about the lack of time you spend with them!

Finally, my friends, who have been supportive of every idea, no matter how crazy!

The benefits

» Freedom to decide how to spend each day.
» Opportunities to meet a wide variety of people, and develop long-lasting business relationships.
» Meeting and sharing knowledge and tips with other free agents!

The drawbacks

» Facing loneliness and challenges to your self-discipline each day.
» The "not knowing where the next check is coming from" syndrome!
» The tremendous effort to be creative and reinvent yourself constantly to suit each different client's needs.

» In my case, to build something from scratch, and to trust that my instincts will show me the way.
» Not fitting in with other people's timetables or budgets for socializing.
» Having to wait for potential clients to find the budget or make a decision on your proposal!

My success factors

The conditions I have chosen to impose upon myself in achieving my success are: that I live with love, honesty, integrity, compassion, and humor every day. By living true to myself each day, I will cultivate the seeds for growth towards the goals I set.

> "Freedom of choice is one good reason to be self-employed. I choose whom I will work for or not. It's good to say no sometimes and not worry."
>
> *Caricaturist Kid Cardona, owner of The Infamous Cartoon*
> *Posse in Austin, Texas*

KEY INSIGHTS

» Cash flow is king.
» Soften the financial peaks and valleys.
» Being serious and treating it as a business.
» Creating a business base close to home.
» Not relying on one customer.
» Charge twice as much as you think you should.
» Charge by the project and not by the hour.
» Keep all intellectual rights to your creations.
» Stay active.
» Choose who you work for.

Key Concepts and Thinkers

Free agency has its own language. This chapter explains some of the terms found in free agency such as IR35, subbies, teleworking, and squirrels.

» Glossary of free agency terms
» Reviewing the literature

"Compared to full-time employees freelancers can save you money (you don't have to pay for insurance, benefits, office space or supplies) and they let you adjust staffing levels more flexibly."

Cheryl Heinonen

GLOSSARY OF FREE AGENCY TERMS

ATSCo – Association of Technology Staffing Companies.

Benchmarking – – Comparing staff needs with data from the market and from direct competitors – areas of good practice.

Brand You – A concept advocated by Bruce Tulgan, among others, whereby a free agent sees themselves as a product and sells themselves accordingly.

Cheetahs – Free agents who reckon they can move fast enough to avoid tangling with IR35 or IRS 1706.

Critical illness cover – Insurance for free agents to provide money if they should become so seriously ill that they couldn't work.

Downsizing – Getting rid of workers to make a business tighter and more profitable.

Eagles – Free agents who have moved beyond the problems of IR35 or IRS 1706 by diversifying and changing direction swiftly.

E-business – A business run entirely over the Web.

E-commerce – Business transactions which take place over the Internet.

E-lancer – Someone who sells their free agency services via the Internet.

ESPP – Employee stock purchase plan.

E-tirement – Occupation of free agents who have reached retirement age but carry on working over the Internet.

Flexi-work – Choosing when one works rather than having fixed hours.

Foxes – Free agents who know all about IR35 or IRS 1706 and are using devious means to avoid the issue such as working under assumed names or being paid in cash.

Free agent – A worker who sells their services/knowledge/skills to a company on a project by project basis.

Freelancers – See free agents.

Guilds – A meeting place for free agents to discuss working conditions, problems encountered, and to share success stories. A mutual back-up society.

Hump management – Hiring in knowledge workers to get a company over a particular hump or crisis or to complete a project.

Independent professionals – See free agents.

INS – Immigration and Naturalization Service in the US – important if you are an Indian software worker seeking work in the US.

IR35 – UK tax ruling which outlines that a worker may be interpreted as a full-time employee rather than a free agent.

IRS 1706 – American tax legislation aimed at defining free agents as full-time employees – see IR35.

IT – Information technology.

Job-for-life – A job that lasted all of one's working career, now extinct.

Just-in-time hiring – Hiring workers as and when a project demands them.

Lions – Free agents who know all about IR35 or IRS 1706 and are taking action forming limited companies, leaving the country (see Cheetahs), setting up service companies, ducking and diving.

Micropreneurs – A small (not in physical size but in size of company) entrepreneur.

Moles – Free agents who have never heard of IR35 or IRS 1706.

Net marketing – Marketing a product or person over the Internet.

Networking – Talking to other free agents over the Internet or other medium.

Ostriches – Free agents who have heard of IR35 or IRS 1706 but are ignoring the issue.

Performance-based remuneration – Being paid by results, being paid by performance rather than logging hours worked.

Permatemps – Temporary workers who have stayed with one organisation so long they are to all intents and purposes really full-time workers.

Recruitment agency – An employment agency that puts free agents and corporations in touch with each other.

Resume – A brief outline and history of a person's working career.

Rightsizing – See downsizing.

Sheep - Free agents who know all about IR35 or IRS 1706 but reckon their financial advisors will solve all problems for them.

Short-term contract - A contract of employment for a short period of time, usually project-based.

SoHo - Small office, home office.

Squirrels - Free agents who know all about IR35 or IRS 1706 and are squirreling away money just in case they have to pay more tax.

Subbies - Sub-contracted workers.

Techies - Information technology workers.

Temp agencies - Employment agencies which supply temporary workers to companies.

Unschooling - Individual-centered learning, like home-schooling and apprenticeships.

Wolves - Inland Revenue/Internal Revenue inspectors who seek to capture more taxation from free agents by way of IR35 or IRS 1706.

REVIEWING THE LITERATURE

Throughout this book we've looked at some of the key players and the major concepts behind free agency. We've also looked at the sort of Websites that will be useful to both prospective free agents and corporations and companies looking to employ them. Now it is time we reviewed the literature. There is a lot out there and we've selected the best of the bunch for you - look no further.

Tom Peters

(1999) *The Brand You50: Or: Fifty Ways to Transform Yourself from an "Employee" into a Brand That Shouts Distinction, Commitment, and Passion!* Alfred Knopf, New York.

Tom Peters uses his essential 50 point plan to show you how to be committed to your goals, choose the right projects for you, improve your networking, and turn yourself into an important commodity. He calls this Brand You.

The book contains 50 ways to brand yourself, along with the sort of resources you'll need - building your Rolodex, crafting your image - that sort of thing. It also sets out to transform your skills portfolio.

Tom Peters continues to be in constant demand for lectures and seminars. In addition to researching and writing his books, he travels more widely than ever to monitor the business environment world-wide. The founder of the Tom Peters Group in Palo Alto, California, he lives mostly on American Airlines, or with his family on an island off the Massachusetts coast or on a farm in Vermont.

Also by Tom Peters:

(1999) *The Project50 (Reinventing Work): Fifty Ways to Transform Every "Task" into a Project That Matters!* Alfred Knopf, New York;

(1999) *The Professional Service Firm50: Or, Fifty Ways to Transform Your "Department" into a Professional Service Firm Whose Trademarks Are Passion and Innovation!* Alfred Knopf, New York;

(1982) *In Search of Excellence: Lessons from America's Best-Run Companies.* Warner Books, New York;

(1994) *The Pursuit of Wow!: Every Person's Guide to Topsy-Turvy Times.* Vintage Books, New York; and

(1987) *Thriving on Chaos: Handbook for a Management Revolution.* Alfred Knopf, New York.

Bruce Tulgan

(2001) *Winning the Talent Wars.* Nicholas Brealey Publishing Ltd, London.

This is a good book for managers who are increasingly trying to get work done in an age of Flexi-staff. It covers all the usual free agency topics and aims to turn managers into productive and competitive hirers.

Management guru Bruce Tulgan, a highly sought-after consultant on staffing issues and author of *Managing Generation X*, the classic study of Generation X in the workplace, offers his six principles of staffing in today's work environment. This book will fundamentally change the way managers think about building a team of talented workers.

The book discusses the vitality of the rise of free-agent employment, in which talented employees negotiate contracts and move from firm to firm, upsetting the traditional order of employment relationships. It also brings to light case studies of how managers are dealing with this situation.

Bruce Tulgan is founder and president of RainmakerThinking, Inc., a management training and consulting firm that researches the working lives of those born after 1963.

Also by Bruce Tulgan:

(2000) *Just in Time Leadership: Managing the Free Agent Workforce*. HRD Books, Amhurst, MA;

(2000) *Career Skills for the New Economy*. HRD Books, Amhurst, MA;

(1998) *Strategic Employee Polls: The Step-By-Step Guide to Discovering What Your Employees Are Really Thinking*. HRD Books, Amhurst, MA;

(1997) *The Manager's Pocket Guide to Generation X*. HRD Press, Amherst, MA; and

(1996) *Managing Generation X: How to Bring Out the Best in Young Talent*. Capstone, Oxford.

Dan Pink

(2001) *Free Agent Nation: How America's New Independent Workers Are Transforming the Way We Live*. Warner Books, New York.

The Organization Man is history. Taking his place is America's new economic icon: the "free agent" – the job-hopping, tech-savvy, fulfillment-seeking self-employed independent worker. Already 30 million strong, these new "disorganization" men and women are transforming America in ways both profound and exhilarating.

In this landmark book, Daniel H. Pink offers the definitive account of this revolution in work. He shows who these free agents are – from the marketing consultant down the street to the home-based mompreneur to the footloose technology contractor – and why they've forged this new path. His entertaining and provocative account of the new frontier of work reveals how America's independent workers are shaking up all our institutions – from politics to education to the family.

KEY CONCEPTS AND THINKERS **69**

This book includes:

» **The Peter-Out Principle** Successor to the famous "Peter Principle", this new rule decrees that when the fun peters out, the talented walk out.
» **Unschooling** Individual-centered learning like home-schooling and apprenticeships will threaten Ivy League colleges and end high school as we know it.
» **Individual Public Offerings** The upper echelon of free agents will issue these new "IPOs", or stock . . . in themselves.
» **E-tirement** When Americans reach age 65, more will enter this new stage of life. Working as full-time, part-time, and anytime free agents, they'll be finding and executing work over the Internet.
» **Just-in-time Politics** The political version of just-in-time manufacturing that will challenge the present two-party system.
» **The Feminine Century** It's here: many analysts estimate that by the year 2005, half of all businesses will be run by women.

Dan Pink is a contributing editor at *Fast Company* magazine. His articles on technology, economic transformation, and the future have appeared in *The New York Times*, *The Washington Post*, *New Republic*, and *Salon*, among others. A former White House speechwriter, Pink lives in Washington, DC with his wife and their two daughters.

Marion McGovern & Dennis Russell

(2000) *A New Brand of Expertise, How Independent Consultants, Free Agents, and Interim Managers are Transforming the World of Work*. Butterworth-Heinemann, London.

This book looks at the enormous benefits to companies and independent consultants of the booming "free agent" marketplace. It clarifies the dynamics of the transaction, including how companies can leverage this highly experienced breed of professionals on a project or interim basis, and how consultants can better position themselves for success. It gives plenty of case studies and practical advice, and explains how this new brand of workers can help solve vital business problems, now more than ever.

It looks at the benefits available to both businesses and employees in the transactions between free agents, interim managers, independent consultants, and the hiring company. It clarifies the dynamics of the situation, from the perspective of the company and the independent consultant, showing the mutual benefits of the relationship.

Gil E. Gordon

(2001) *Turn It Off: How to Unplug from the Anytime-Anywhere Office Without Disconnecting Your Career*. Nicholas Brealey Publishing Ltd, London.

We check e-mail on the weekend or late at night, answer pagers at all hours, send faxes from home, work while we're on vacation – all because we can. It's out of control. This book sets out to show how we can reclaim the boundaries between work life and personal life and still excel at our jobs and maintain our professional livelihoods.

It is full of practical advice, *Turn It Off* will show you how to regain control and obtain a sense of balance between the very real demands of today's business world and your personal need to get – and really live – a life. It includes topics such as:

» self-tests for evaluating how much your work and personal time overlap;
» methods for managing e-mail and voice mail so they don't control you;
» advice on getting your clients and your boss to respect your boundaries; and
» suggestions for what to do if you're the boss – and why "unplugging" is good for business.

It is all based on the "100/60/0" model for balancing time and work – a method to help you figure out when you'll be "on" and available to the office 100% of the time, part of the time, or not at all. A good book if you want to make changes to the way computers control our lives. A good read if you are ready to turn it off and take back control.

The author states that his goals are:

» to help you hold a mirror up to your life and see how mobile-office technology may have changed your work habits and your life;

» to let you look at that assessment and make some deliberate decisions about how you might re-establish some boundaries between work and the rest of life; and

» to equip you to develop a specific plan for doing so, and for taking this plan to your boss and/or co-workers and clients and gaining their support – without getting fired or losing business.

This book won't solve all your work – or home – problems, it won't make you love a job you otherwise hate, and it won't forever free you from the electronic tethers of voice mail and e-mail. But if you want to create a more balanced and enjoyable lifestyle, this book is for you.

Gil Gordon is a telecommuting and virtual-office guru who has been featured in publications ranging from the *Wall Street Journal* to *USA Today* for his work worldwide with clients such as Citicorp, AT&T, and Merrill Lynch. He lives in Monmouth Junction, New Jersey.

Thomas H. Davenport & John C. Beck

(2001) The Attention Economy: Understanding the New Currency of Business. Harvard Business School Press, Boston, MA.

This is a good managerial and executive guide to important aspects of the economy and the data-driven, electronically-advancing marketplace. An exposition of how paying attention really works in the knowledge economy, showing how to clarify what is really important for any organization.

Thomas H. Davenport is the Director of the Accenture Institute for Strategic Change and a Distinguished Scholar in Residence at Babson College. He is the author of *Mission Critical: Realizing the Promise of Enterprise Systems*, *Process Innovation: Reengineering Work through Information Technology*, and the co-author of *Working Knowledge: How Organizations Manage What They Know*.

John C. Beck is a Senior Research Fellow at the Accenture Institute for Strategic Change and a Visiting Professor at the Anderson School of Management at UCLA.

Richard Donkin

(2001) *Blood, Sweat and Tears: The Evolution of Work*. Texere
Publishing, New York.

A good narrative history of work – and the individuals and events
that have been responsible for its evolution. Work has radically changed
over the centuries. Most of these changes have involved revolutionary
steps, significantly influencing the way people live and behave. Two
of these – the agrarian revolution and the industrial revolution – were
watersheds in the evolution of work. A third revolution is occurring
now in the way we work and live, driven this time by new technology.
This is a popular history of work, from prehistoric times to the present
day. It offers fascinating and intelligent analyses of the individuals,
assumptions, theories, developments, and events that have changed
work.

Richard Donkin is a leading columnist and writer for the *Financial
Times*, specializing in work and management topics. He is currently on
assignment with FT.com. He regularly appears on radio and contributes
to other leading magazines on issues relating to business. He lives in
the UK.

Resources

Free agency is a fast-moving modern phenomenon. A lot is currently being written on the subject and this chapter lists the best resources, including a summary of useful Websites.

- » Working Today
- » Monster Talent Market
- » FreeAgentNation
- » Votech Education
- » Free Agent.com
- » Guru
- » Job hunter
- » HR consultants
- » Fast Company
- » IT Contracting
- » Unicomsystems

"By the year 2010, half of all Americans will be in 'new century, new economy' (a.k.a. 'free agent') jobs."

PBS Career Center for Texas

WORKING TODAY

Working Today's service package includes access to health insurance for independent workers and their families, 30 minutes of free legal advice from practitioners with expertise in every area of the law, and discounts on dental care, natural health/alternative care, computers, and office equipment and supplies. Please note that new membership benefits are continually being developed, so you should check out this site on a regular basis: http://www.workingtoday.org/

Working Today is a national non-profit membership organisation that promotes the interests of people who work independently – a diverse group that now makes up nearly 30% of the American Labor force. Their members are freelancers, independent contractors, temps, part-timers, contingent workers, and people working from home.

Working Today takes a three-pronged approach to promoting the interests of the independent workforce-service, education, and advocacy.

Working Today publication

Read Working Today's just-released report *Mobile Workers, Immobile Health Benefits: The State of Independent Work*.

Working Today projects

Working Today is especially grateful to New York State Assembly Speaker Sheldon Silver, who represents downtown Manhattan, for his support of a State grant for the Silicon Alley Portable Benefits Network. The project will offer Silicon Alley independent workers cost-effective health, life, and disability insurance beginning later this summer.

If you work in New York City's new media or high-tech industries and need access to health, life, and disability insurance or if you'd like to be contacted when Benefits Network enrollment begins then email Working Today at membership@workingtoday.org.

Working Today in the news:

"Using that premise (that benefits need to be tied to the individual), Horowitz is attempting nothing less than an overhaul of the rules of labor."
Susan Caminiti "Independents Day". Kinko's IMPRESS (Forbes Special Interest Publication), Issue 5, 2001

"In a workforce where more and more people are becoming free agents ... our Labor laws are becoming as outdated as a Kaypro computer. America's next secretary of Labor will have to reckon with the rise of Free Agent Nation – which is why [Fast Company] would like to nominate Sara Horowitz, the savvy founder of Working Today, America's premier free-agent advocacy group."
Daniel H. Pink "Fast.Gov". Fast Company, October 2000

"The MacArthur genius finders have already embraced the far-sighted Sara Horowitz, the founder and leader of Working Today ... The reward [of effective representation for independent workers] will be benefits collectively achieved and individually coded ... "
Max Frankel "Free Agents Unite!". The New York Times Magazine, March 5, 2000

In June 1999, the MacArthur Foundation named Sara Horowitz, founder and executive director of Working Today, one of its 32 fellows for the year. Candidates for this award, commonly known as a "genius" grant, are nominated by prominent figures representing a variety of fields; an anonymous panel chooses the recipients.

Adele Simmons, president of the MacArthur Foundation, said of the 1999 winners: "The 1999 class of Fellows is full of creative people doing unusual and important things in a broad range of disciplines. They are transforming and bridging fields, making major breakthroughs, illuminating responsibility for humanity's inhumanities, solving persistent contemporary problems, and expanding our imagination about what is possible."

MONSTER TALENT MARKET

Monster Talent Market – Talentmarket.monster.com – is the world's first online, auction-style marketplace that connects free agents with companies and organisations requiring talent on a contract basis. Launched by Monster.com in July 1999, the service provides for real-time searches of detailed free agent profiles. These profiles can be matched with the talent requirements of projects that companies and organizations post.

Monster Talent Market attracts a diverse pool of contract talent that can include, for example, management consultants, project accountants, graphic designers, IT programmers, etc. Through their profiles, free agents can market their skills and experience directly to employers for short- and long-term assignments. The Monster Talent Market site also provides leading-edge content that informs and supports free agents as they exercise their value in this burgeoning market space.

Companies, on the other hand, utilize the service to fill contract assignments quickly and effectively, by placing bids on prospective talent. To make the initial match, searches can be defined according to profession, location, availability, whether talent is required on-site or off-site, and any relevant keywords.

Contacts

» To learn more about Monster Talent Market: talentmarket@monster.com
» To explore alliance and partnering opportunities: dwight@monster.com
» For public relations inquiries: dean.rosingana@monster.com

FREEAGENTNATION

About FreeAgentNation.com

In late 1998 FreeAgentNation.com was launched – a non-commercial Website and e-newsletter for independent workers.

Over the last two years, much has changed. Free agency has taken deeper root in American life – as a reality and an aspiration. America's soloists and micropreneurs have earned new respect. Dozens of start-up companies have exploded onto the scene to serve the emerging market of independent workers. And their own modest site has begun attracting some 10,000 visitors a month – while their newsletter subscribers have climbed from several dozen to several thousand.

All of this is great news. But it also means they believe they've got to change with the times. That's why they've been working on FreeAgentNation.com 2.0 – a revamped and re-energized version of this site which was launched in the spring of 2001.

VOTECH EDUCATION

In February of 1997, Scott Kurnit and a dedicated team launched The Mining Company, the first information network to integrate the Internet's most productive agent – people. The company quickly grew in size and scale and in 1999 the company was renamed About, to reflect its breadth of content, services and ease of use. Today, About is visited by one in five online users each month, making it one of the most popular destinations on the Net.

Who are the About Guides?

Coming from different backgrounds and from all over the world, About Guides know their subjects as well as anyone. Together they have gathered and created hundreds of thousands of pages of content to share with users. Whether they're providing insight and guidance, initiating discussions, moderating chats or writing articles, it is their knowledge, commitment, and passion that enable About to provide their millions of regular users with the most human online experience.

About Guides live and work in over 20 countries and celebrate their interests in over 700 topics. Guides are selected for their ability to provide the most interesting information for users, their commitment to finding the best sites, and for their passion for their subject and the Net. They include a lot of extremely useful information on free agency including:

» Free Agents;
» Are You Ready to Become a Free Agent?;
» Tips on Going Solo;
» Education Resources for Free Agents;

» Free Agent Web Sites and Information Resources;
» Contracting Agencies for Free Agents;
» Free Agent Associations & Organizations;
» Guidance & Information for Free Agents;
» Free Agent Services & Helpful Places;
» Financial/Legal/Medical Resources for Free Agents;
» Success Stories from Free Agents; and
» Related About.com Sites.

Contact

» http://www.About.com/education/votech

FREE AGENT.COM

For a brave new workforce

Corporations have downsized. They've relocated. They've merged. They've taught us that long-term loyalty counts for far less than profit and flexibility.

And we have all learned from their example. The workforce is reinventing itself. Millions of men and women are choosing to become consultants, freelancers, independent contractors – professional free agents. As a free agent, you decide how to blend work and life. You choose where to work, for how long, what you'll do, and how much you'll be paid. You can place health, wealth, and happiness over boring meetings, office politics, and skimpy raises. You can get the control, independence, and options that come with being your own boss.

It's time to be paid what you're worth. It's time to put stock in yourself, bet on your abilities, explore what you can create. It's time to be judged on your skills and your results. Say goodbye to the boss. Say hello to freedom.

Welcome to FreeAgent.com. They're glad you're there and they hope you'll join them in building the largest and most useful network of free agents on and off the Internet. They started FreeAgent.com to help you leave the rickety corporate framework behind for good. Their mission: To help free agents achieve long-term wealth, success, and a balanced life.

They're there to help you:

» make more money for now and your future;
» build your business and enjoy more free time;
» be free to make your own decisions;
» test out ideas, vent frustrations;
» belong to a vital, networked, supportive community; and
» do work you really love.

They don't pretend to have all the answers, but they think they're on the right track. If you don't see it here, let them know what you want and they'll try to make it happen!

Contact
» http://www.Freeagent.com

GURU

All over the world, millions of ambitious professionals are heading out on their own. They work as Web designers or Linux programmers, strategists or public relations specialists, writers or virtual CEOs. They describe themselves as consultants, freelancers, moonlighters, or hired guns. Their clients are Fortune 500 corporations, local businesses, fast-moving start-ups, and anyone anywhere who needs serious brainpower.

Guru, Inc. is the world's most powerful independent professional talent resource. The company offers three core services. Guru is the leading online marketplace connecting freelancers and consultants with contract projects from companies who source their contingent talent on the Web. Ranked the top project marketplace on the Web by sources including *PC Magazine*, *Yahoo! Internet Life*, *Forbes.com*, *PC Data*, and *Media Metrix*, Guru has over 550,000 registered users. Through Guru Talent Agency, Guru pre-screens and represents top-flight IT and creative contractors, and places them into projects with companies who need full-service talent placement. Guru's third division, Guru Services, provides independent professionals with essential services, such as insurance, to run their solo businesses. Guru, Inc. has raised $63mn in financing from investors including Greylock, August Capital, Investor AB, CS First Boston, American Express, WR Hambrecht, Red

Hat, and Texas Pacific Group. Founded in April 1999, the company is headquartered in San Francisco, California.

Guru is dedicated to empowering independent professionals and the clients who hire them. To take advantage of everything Guru has to offer, all you have to do is register. (Don't panic, registration is free!) Then, stop by from time to time to see how they can help you get more work done – faster and easier.

Contact

» http://www.Guru.com

JOB HUNTER

Texastechjobs.com is an online recruiting service specializing in assisting highly skilled professionals in the technical employment markets in the State of Texas.

In addition, they offer high-tech industries a reliable, cost-saving alternative to in-house recruiting. As a true alternative to in-house recruiting they offer a very high level of practical experience, know-how, contacts, and confidentiality.

Clients know that working with Texastechjobs.com is a more professional, time-saving way to locate and hire the right people without tying up internal resources.

For free agents looking for work this site includes:

» Job Hunter's Tool Kit;
» Post your resume;
» Search a Job Database;
» MEGA Job Search;
» Featured Jobs Showcase;
» Freelance Registry;
» Hot Job News; and
» Tell a Friend.

And for employers seeking talent:

» Employer's Tool Kit;
» Post your open positions;
» Search our Resume Database;

» Search for Freelance Talent; and
» Partner Extranet Sign-in.

Contact

» http://www.texastechjobs.com/index.html

HR CONSULTANTS

PersonnelToday.com is a high value, free access site which gives HR and personnel professionals access to the archives of *Personnel Today*, *Training*, and *Employers' Law* magazines. In addition to this wealth of unique, essential data, the site features up-to-the-minute HR news, information about HR jobs, careers advice, and an impressive directory of suppliers of HR products and services.

Contact

» http://www.personneltoday.co.uk

FAST COMPANY

What Is *Fast Company?*

Launched in November 1995 by Alan Webber and Bill Taylor, two former *Harvard Business Review* editors, *Fast Company* magazine was founded on a single premise: A global revolution was changing business, and business was changing the world. Discarding the old rules of business, *Fast Company* set to chronicle how changing companies create and compete, to highlight new business practices, and to showcase the teams and individuals who are inventing the future and reinventing business.

Now dozens of issues – and awards – later *Fast Company* is more than a magazine: it's a movement. It's a series of engaging live events. It's an acclaimed Website. It's a global community. Together, these components strive to help people in the new economy discover the tools, techniques, and tactics they need to succeed at work and life.

About fastcompany.com

Fastcompany.com extends the *Fast Company* experience to the Web. Specifically, the site serves people's individual career needs with six custom-built Career Zones. Each Career Zone contains Web-only stories, interactive tools, expert opinions, and valuable connections to help *Fast Company* readers get ahead in the new economy.

» Build Your Business – Resources and advice for growing your business.
» Lead Your Team – Tools for recruiting, managing, and developing your team.
» Go Solo – Resources and connections for independent professionals.
» Reinvent Yourself – Tools for relaunching your career in the new economy.
» Launch Your Career – Essentials for mastering the new world of work.
» Be a Change Agent – Community support and best practices for corporate fire starters.

Their other features include the complete magazine archives online, the Company of Friends, the Fast Take newsletter, and the FC: Forums, among others. For a complete list of their site offerings, visit their site guide.

Contact

» http://www.fastcompany.com

IT CONTRACTING

Itcontracting.com is a really useful site that works as an online resource center for IT professionals and brings you a range of information – from the best job search engines to a list of recruitment agencies to pertinent articles on issues of interest to IT professionals. It also has a variety of interesting and useful articles to help both free agents and those corporations seeking to employ them. Their titles include:

» Editorial Features – Career Development;
» How to set yourself up as an IT Contractor;
» Five job interview mistakes;
» Seven essential laws of marketing yourself;
» Making your resume work for you;

» The pros and cons of contracting in the public sector;
» The fine art of renegotiation;
» What's the best strategy?;
» When marketing yourself matters?
» Picking a winning team;
» How to build a team of hardworking, focused individuals;
» Should You Stay or Should You Leave?;
» Thinking about leaving your job and moving into another role?;
» Managing Conflicts in a Project;
» Interface Designers for the Web – A New Breed;
» 10 reasons why you did not get the contract;
» From a Permanent Worker to a Contractor – What you need to Know;
» Flexible work options – the lifestyle you've always wanted;
» Steps to better communication skills;
» You're a contractor but now you want to go back to a full-time role;
» Constant Employment – Marketing Yourself;
» Cultivating Meaningful Relationships – Identifying those who can help you;
» Using an IT Expo To Get Your Next Contract;
» Fitting in With the Culture of the Place;
» Choosing an IT Recruiter;
» A Question of Balance – The Ideal Project Manager;
» How to Determine your Rates;
» What Commission Should Agencies Be On – You Decide!'
» What is Your Hourly Rate?; and
» Power Packed Resumes.

Contact:

» http://www.Itcontracting.com

UNICOMSYSTEMS

Technologies' most important resources are natural – Human Resources.

It should go without saying that IT wouldn't exist without the people who create it. Yet the demanding IT industry can be dehumanizing if you feel you're in the wrong job, or you find yourself without a job, or indeed, without the person you need for the job.

At Unicom, they treat IT's natural resources with care and respect: they consider them people, not products.

You may also like to visit their Gateway to employment opportunities in Asia: http://www.ucom.com.my/

Contact

» http://www.unicomsystems.com

Ten Steps to Making Free Agency Work

Free agency theory is fine but it has to be made to work in practice. This chapter provides the key insights into the practical aspects of free agency.

1 Making the move
2 Making it work
3 Have a plan
4 Research the market
5 Protect yourself
6 Get paid
7 Manage your cash flow
8 Safeguard your money from the tax office
9 Be motivated
10 Sell yourself

"The essence of working solo is to embark on a path of self-discovery through entrepreneurship. It's the freedom to craft the life you want to live."

Terri Lonier, president of Working Solo Inc. in San Francisco, author of Working Solo: The Real Guide to Freedom and Financial Success with Your Own Business

1. MAKING THE MOVE

So you've finally made the decision – you're going it alone. You are going to be a free agent and sell your services, your skills, your information, your knowledge, your talents – and all to the highest bidder. Before you can start to get work you need to do some preparation beforehand.

» Know your skills or knowledge – exactly what is it you are trying to sell?
» Put together a decent resume – short, succinct, informative, clear, eye-catching.
» Make sure you reach the widest audience possible – through net marketing, signing up with a recruitment agency, – whatever.
» Make sure you are ready for interview – good communication skills, adequate preparation, a knowledge of the company you are applying to, – that sort of thing.
» Being ready to discuss/negotiate rates, contracts, etc.

When you launch yourself as a free agent you will need to make sure that certain things are ever-present in your attitude and approach:

» professionalism;
» confidence;
» experience;
» honesty;
» confidentiality;
» energy; and
» enthusiasm.

Professionalism

You've got to be able to walk your talk. You have to deliver the goods on time and correctly done. Always imagine yourself as an ambassador for all other free agents. Don't let people down. If you promise a job will be done, then make sure it is done. Strive to maintain complete and utter professionalism in everything you do – you'll quickly get a bad reputation if you don't.

Confidence
Firm handshake, good eye contact – that sort of thing. Look and sound as if you know what you are doing at all times. If you have confidence in yourself it will inspire others to have confidence in you.

Experience
If you haven't got it, you don't have to admit that. There's no point lying about your experience (see ''Honesty'' below) but you don't have to tell them everything you don't know or haven't done. A little bullshit never hurt anyone's career. If you have the confidence mentioned above you can carry it off. And if you do have the experience then make sure you let them know.

Honesty
Don't tell lies. Not about anything. You'll be found out at some time so don't start, don't take the risk. If you have a skill to sell then don't lie about it. You can embellish a little, bullshit a lot, but don't tell lies. Be honest in your dealings with everyone and you'll sleep better at nights.

Confidentiality
When you work for a company you learn secrets. When you go to work for that company's competitors, keep what you know to yourself. Once you get a reputation as someone everyone can trust you get more work.

Energy
You will need to work a lot harder than someone in a steady job, so make sure you eat right, sleep right and have enough energy to carry the day. Be ready to put in more hours, longer hours, harder hours and you will be successful.

Enthusiasm
Approach everything you do with enthusiasm. If you ain't enjoying it, quit. If you do enjoy it then communicate that to others around you. Let your smile be infectious and your approach to work be fun.

2. MAKING IT WORK

A free agency which fails can cost you your savings, and sometimes even your house. But how can you be sure that your new free agency business will succeed? The answer is to plan, plan, plan.

Business advice network

Small free agency businesses which take professional advice are more likely to succeed than those which don't. Some free agents seem to see asking for advice as an admission of failure, but in fact it is a sign of a smart free agent. Knowing how to use business advisors is a valuable skill in itself. You can't possibly be an expert in every area of business, but fortunately there are plenty of organizations which can fill in the gaps in your own experience. And remember that being a free agent isn't just going it alone – you are in business, are running a business, and have a business.

Once you know where to go, you can easily obtain advice on specialist disciplines such as business planning, marketing, exporting, financial management, grants and funding, IT, training, innovation and design, and management development. The important points to follow when you're looking for outside advice for your free agency are:

» make sure you choose the right advisor;
» know how to get the best from your advisor;
» seek advice at every stage, starting before you even set your free agency up; and
» don't leave it too late or wait until you hit a crisis before you get advice.

Four steps to getting the best from your business advisor.

1 Choose the right advisor for your free agency: Find someone who suits you and your business, and who you can all get along with. And make sure you've picked the right expert. For example, do you need a PR specialist or a general marketing advisor?
2 Make sure your expectations are reasonable: Solutions are rarely as quick and easy as you might hope, so expect some hard work before you see the results you want.

3 Tell the advisor everything they need to know: No one can work effectively if they don't have all the facts. If you want to get the best advice, you must tell the advisor everything relevant, including your weaknesses and failures.

4 Be prepared to put in your own time: An advisor's job is to work with you, not go away and solve your problems in isolation. They will expect you to contribute to analyzing the problem and developing the solution.

Business advice network – contacts

Business Link is a UK network of contacts which gives you access to all sorts of reliable business advice, services, and information, much of it non-commercial. Your Personal Business Advisor will discuss your requirements and put you in touch with the best organization to help you. Business Link partner organizations include:

» enterprise agencies, which offer advice (often free) for anyone starting up their own business;
» Training and Enterprise Councils (TECs), known in Scotland as Local Enterprise Councils (LECs), which are private, independent companies led by local business people. They offer advice, support and training;
» Chambers of Commerce, the voice of local business, which offer international trade information, training, and cost-effective commercial services; and
» local authorities, which can help with local advice such as bye-laws, planning queries and public services.

For other help, contact your bank manager or independent financial advisor, who can direct you to the nearest source of business advice.

3. HAVE A PLAN

It's better to find out now that your idea is not viable – or viable only if you modify it – than to wait until the free agency is up and running and losing you a fortune.

There are several key areas you need to plan when starting up a free agency, and your business plan should incorporate them all; this is why a business plan is essential. If you need help putting a business plan together, your independent financial advisor can help you and direct you to other sources of support and advice. In particular, you need to research and plan:

» your service or skill or talent or knowledge;
» your customers;
» your marketing;
» your pricing; and
» your finances.

4. RESEARCH THE MARKET

Make sure there is a market.

» Consider using a research questionnaire, whether you conduct it by phone, post, or face-to-face. You can use market research to help establish attitudes to services, to pricing, to methods of working or location, and to all sorts of other variables.
» Research books, newspapers and industry reports, trade journals, trade show catalogues, competitors' brochures, magazines, the Internet, and many other sources.

Many banks and independent financial advisors produce business information fact sheets on market research questionnaires and on sources of market and business information.

Don't underestimate the importance of the pricing plan.

» Don't assume it's best to be cheap. Sometimes low prices are best, but they will cut your profit margins. And sometimes customers don't believe in quality unless it is reflected in the price.
» ... but price competitively. Find out what the competition is charging. Unless your customers want to pay more for a better service, you risk pricing yourself out of the market.
» Ensure you can make a profit or you will go out of business. Only careful planning will ensure that your gross margins will cover all your overheads and expenses and still leave you with a profit.

How do you know that your services are wanted? Or needed? And how do you place yourself competitively in the marketplace? Perhaps some simple market research could help. Market research has four vital functions:

1 to monitor the changes in how your customers see you and what they want from you – and the companies and corporations are your customers;
2 to explore the reasons behind a problem;
3 to identify new markets for your services; and
4 to identify new services for your market.

The more tightly you target your market, the more efficiently you will be spending your money. So if you haven't much money to start with, market research is vital – and the more thorough the better.

Whether you are starting up a new free agency business or running a long established one, you are going to have to research your market. If your free agency business has been going a long time, it's easy to think you know the answers already. But it's not as simple as that. The market is constantly changing, and you need to research that change to make sure you develop alongside it.

The real difference between marketing and non-marketing companies is the ability to change. Free agents will always leave, companies go bust, people move out of the area, they prefer your competitors – so you need to recruit new customers all the time simply to stand still. You need to work even harder if you want to grow. And the market's always changing; what's right today will be wrong tomorrow. So you need to keep researching it.

A lot of people go weak at the knees at the prospect of doing their own research. They avoid the mere thought of it, for the perfectly good reason that they haven't the first idea how to go about it. In fact, there are three key types of information.

» *Ready-made information*: for example libraries, trade associations, government departments, regulatory bodies, local enterprise agencies, trade press.
» *Your own records*: knowing what existing customers do and don't want from you, what they will pay, how often they require your services, what they complain about and so on, gives you hefty clues as to how future customers will behave.

» *New information*: telephone, fax, and postal questionnaires to existing customers, ex-customers, and prospects, asking them the questions to which you need answers, will bring in new information.

By pursuing any or all of these three types of research, you should be able to find out just about anything you need to know to drive your free agency business forward successfully.

5. PROTECT YOURSELF

What would happen to your business if you had to spend a month in hospital? Or if you had a stroke and lost the use of one of your limbs? It may not be pleasant to contemplate, but if you prepare for the worst, at least you don't have to lose your business and your income on top of coping with illness.

Any small free agency business is deeply dependent on one person – you. You are the business. You may be able to afford a few days off, but what happens if you have to take several weeks or even months off work as a result of accident or illness? How can you earn a living if you're not fit enough to work?

Insurance to protect against this sort of thing is essential, and yet many small free agency businesses bury their heads in the sand, thinking it won't happen to them. Critical illness cover gives you a lump sum pay-out as soon as you are diagnosed with one of a specific list of illnesses. These usually include:

» cancer;
» heart attack/coronary bypass surgery;
» kidney failure;
» major organ transplant;
» multiple sclerosis; and
» stroke.

Some critical illness policies also insure you for other conditions such as Alzheimer's disease, diabetes, blindness, and sometimes HIV.

6. GET PAID

When you're running a small free agency business, one of the greatest worries is dealing with companies who don't pay on time. But it's a problem you have to get to grips with, or it can literally bankrupt you.

A lot of free agents feel uncomfortable about chasing up debts. After all, you badly need to keep on the right side of your customers, and the prospect of ringing them up and giving them a hard time seems like completely the wrong approach. But in fact, so long as you handle it the right way, they will recognize that you are simply doing your job. It gives you a professional image, which is no bad thing.

Here are a few tips for making debt collection easier.

» Invoice as soon as a job is done. Don't wait until the end of the month. That way, however long the customer takes to pay, at least if the process starts sooner it will end sooner.

» Make sure you have all the relevant facts to hand. Keep clear records, and check them before you phone to chase payment. That way, you avoid the potential embarrassment of being told that the dates you said you worked don't tally with what they say you worked or that you failed to quote the customer's order number.

» Agree payment terms with your customers, or print them on the back of your contract, so there is no room for dispute over whether payment is actually due.

» Find out what your customers' payment systems are. Do they always pay on the last Tuesday of the month? Or do a check run every Friday?

» Contact your customer a few days *before* the payment becomes due. Explain you have just rung to make sure your invoice arrived, with any order numbers or other requirements included, and that payment is going through.

» Remember that the accounts department and whoever it is that actually employs you are two different things – chances are the person who employs you won't even get to hear that you have been hassling the accounts department.

» If a customer consistently pays late, at least budget for it.

» Sometimes it simply isn't worth keeping a customer if they are really unreliable payers. It takes a lot of courage to turn down work but it can be the best move, financially as well as for the sake of your stress levels.

7. MANAGE YOUR CASH FLOW

Cash flow problems happen when you haven't got enough money to pay the bills, even though the money may be promised or due in, or even overdue. Managing cash flow is an essential part of running a business, and it is a skill that can make or break you. A lot of problems can be avoided in the first place by sticking to certain permanent rules.

» Make sure your payment terms are as beneficial to you as possible.
» Always chase bad debtors promptly, and be firm. Don't take on loads of work from someone who still hasn't paid their last overdue bills.
» Budget for the fact that a proportion of your customers will pay late.
» Pay your creditors when the payment is due, but not before.
» If you have to keep any stocks in the way of raw materials then keep your stock levels to a minimum, otherwise you are tying up money you may need to get at quickly.
» Produce a regular cash flow forecast, and a three-year business plan that covers cash flow and is updated every year.
» Hang onto some surplus funds to cushion you against any major problems such as a substantial bad debt. If you operate with no cash safety net at all, it is only a matter of time before you hit difficulties.

One of the biggest threats to cash flow comes when a customer wants you to work for a long period without invoicing – say getting paid every six months. As a free agent it is obviously impossible for you to do this – perhaps under the umbrella of an employment agency it might be feasible. But you will simply have to turn this work down unless:

» you can negotiate interim payments with your customer; or
» you can arrange a loan with your bank, and build the cost of the interest in to your price to the customer.

Failure to do either of these can bankrupt a business, so if the customer won't agree to it, you might have to turn down the work, painful – and even stupid – though it may seem.

8. SAFEGUARD YOUR MONEY FROM THE TAX OFFICE

We looked at the tax situation in earlier chapters. No matter what a free agent tries to do, the tax office will do all they can to classify them as full-time employees. The reason for this is that as a free agent they are entitled to claim a lot of expenses to be set against profits. Thus they pay less tax. The tax office wants them classified as full-time employees to stop these expenses being claimed and thus they will pay more tax. It's a simple battle and one the free agent will have to partake of – there is no choice. Once someone sets up as a free agent they will encounter this game. Staying one step of the game is what it is all about. Some free agents elect to work via an employment agency to try and circumvent this. Others will work for many corporations in an effort to prove they truly are free agents.

We looked earlier at how free agents can prove their independence.

» Working from home – ideally.
» Presenting invoices for work done rather than going on a payroll.
» Keeping separate business stationery.
» Never working for one single employer for too long – less than six months ideally.
» Choosing when and where they work.
» Not being included in staff pension schemes or other such things.
» Not using a company car – or even one from a company pool.
» Have a clear contract that specifies you are a free agent and not an employee with a definite cut-off date written in.

I think you get the idea – don't get labeled in any way as an employee.

9. BE MOTIVATED

When you become a free agent there ain't nobody gonna get you up and out of bed in the mornings. You have to be motivated. And the only real motivation is no, not money. It helps but it doesn't work the magic. There is only one thing that gets your juices going and that is enjoyment. If you don't enjoy it, don't do it. Being a free agent can be hard work, scary, desperate, and daunting – but it's also meant to be better than sitting in a 9 to 5 office. If you are out there selling yourself, walking your walk, talking your talk, what more can you want? Sure, it gets lonely at times and you get demoralized and down. But at the end of the day you don't have to kowtow to anyone, you don't have to sit up straight or wear a tie. You are free to choose who you work for and when. That is the motivation. Print it out big and set it in front of you for those moments when you wonder what in the hell you thought you were doing when you went solo.

Career prospects I hear you ask? You don't have any. Careers are from the old days when we clocked in and picked up a wage check at the end of the month. A career is a sad plotting along a line of single promotions culminating in early retirement and a golf course. You are a free agent. You have wings and can make leaps of proportions not available to the 9-to-5s. When you go solo you have to have a game plan – this isn't the same thing as a career although it might have similarities. You need to know:

» what you are aiming for;
» what sort of path you think may get you there;
» what the game is all about;
» what sort of game you think you're playing;
» who the other players you choose to play with are;
» how you define winning;
» how you define losing; and
» what the prize is.

Once you have this sort of game plan you know where you are going. But how you get there isn't limited by a career promotion path. You could make it to endgame in a single bound or wallow in the opening rounds for the rest of your working life. Remember you are a free agent – you sell yourself, knowledge, your talents or skills. You do not have to buy into anyone else's reality.

Quick story: a free agent was sitting by the river bank fishing. A businessman in executive limo pulls up and demands to know what he is doing.

"Fishing," replies the free agent. "Why?"

The business man asks: "Haven't you got a proper job?"

"No, I'm a free agent. Why should I have a proper job?"

"Because if you had a proper job you could get on, work your way up the corporate ladder, become a CEO or company chairman – or even president of a large conglomerate."

"And why would I want to do that?"

"Because then you could work what hours suited you, you could take time off when you wanted."

"And what would I do with all that time off?"

"Oh, I don't know," replied the businessman exasperatedly, "you could spend your days fishing."

10. SELL YOURSELF

This is a very important part of being a free agent. If you haven't read Tom Peters'' *The Brand You50*, then get a copy today (see Chapter 8). Basically, what he says is that you have to see yourself as a commodity. Once you've made this mental leap the rest is easy – follow Tom's 50 essential points to become a brand – you.

There are a lot of tins of beans out there sitting on supermarket shelves. They all look the same. They all do the same job. How are you going to get a corporation to pick the tin that is you? You've got to stand out. How you do this is a personal choice. I always tell anyone who wants to buy my writing services – be that as a copywriter, author, press release writer, whatever – that I have three services to offer:

» they can have it quick;
» they can have it cheap;
» they can have it good.

Then I tell them that they can only have two of the three. This makes them laugh and they remember me. It also sets up a dilemma for them as I stick rigidly to it and won't waver. They really do only get two out of the three. You'll have to judge which two the publishers of this title went for.

E-lancing and e-agency

It's big. It's efficient. It's world-wide. It's the Web. Anyone can now be an e-business, online and selling themselves for around $500. By using the Internet you can advertise your services by signing up to any of the many, many free agents' agencies online. You can post your e-resume, apply for jobs online, even be interviewed online. And all from the comfort of your kitchen table or backyard shed.

Putting together a resume

There are a few rules when it comes to putting a resume together. Follow them and you'll get put at the top of the pile. Don't follow them and chances are your resume will end up in File 13 - the wastepaper basket.

» make it short;
» make it simple;
» make it relevant;
» make it clear.

Try to avoid:

» waffle - it's a resume not an autobiography, stick to the detail;
» erroneous detail - so you were basketball captain in junior high - who cares, can you program/design/write/produce results now? That's all that matters;
» too many typefaces - one is fine. You can use **bold** or *italics* or even underlining to tart it up a bit;
» color or fancy graphics - too much time on your hands. Busy free agents are out there working, not playing with their Apple Macs;
» being too jokey - shows an immature mind - apparently; and
» lying - tell the truth about your qualifications and experience - but you can feel free to embellish and bullshit.

Now you're ready to send it out.

Finding work

Easy. You have the knowledge or skill or talent. Out there are many agencies who will post your details to a great number of companies and corporations who are seeking free agents. But there are also many other ways of making contact:

» your former employer;
» trade journals;
» free agent guilds;
» word of mouth;
» previous contacts;
» mail shots; and
» telephone inquiries.

But really, for efficiency, peace of mind, ease of use, and enormous coverage all you have to do is locate the sites that handle your sort of work and supply your details. Here's an example.

WELCOME TO RENT A GEEK

Rent A Geek is one of many good sources for locating freelance computer consultants and consulting companies. Their searchable database will help you find someone in your area that can provide the services you need, quickly and easily.

For computer consultants, Rent A Geek provides detailed listings that are presented to a vast customer base. International advertising, free of charge. Rent A Geek proclaims that they are the Web's leading directory of independent computer consultants. Visitors can search their database by geographical location or by specific skills, or both.

Free listing

There is no charge for placing a full listing with Rent A Geek. Their easy to use, comprehensive registration form makes it simple for professionals to immediately list their services with them.

Tell them what you think

They claim they welcome all comments. So if you've got something to say about the way they run their site or their business – let them know.

END NOTES

Being a free agent isn't a bed of roses, but it can be stimulating, exciting, and motivating. Being out there living by your wits makes you feel alive and independent. We hope this title will have been of considerable use both to those who want to be free agents and to those who are thinking of using them. It's a good relationship when it works well. Good luck and stay free.

Frequently Asked Questions (FAQs)

Q1: What is a free agent?

A: See Chapter 2 – What is Free Agency?

Q2: How do I go about becoming one?

A: See Chapter 3 – The Evolution of the Free Agent.

Q3: What sort of benefits can I expect?

A: See Chapter 7 – In Practice: Free Agent Success Stories.

Q4: What sort of disadvantages are there to being a free agent?

A: See Chapter 7 – In Practice: Free Agent Success Stories.

Q5: What will be my tax position?

A: See Chapter 2 – Section: Free agents and the law.

Q6: How do I find new customers?

A: See Chapter 10 – Ten Steps to Making Free Agency Work.

Q7: Who are the shakers and movers in free agency?

A: See Chapter 8 – Key Concepts and Thinkers.

Q8: Where do I find out more?

A: See Chapter 9 – Resources.

Q9: What are the benefits of using an employment agency?

A: See Chapter 4 – The E-Dimension.

Q10: Will I be happier as a free agent?

A: See Chapter 1 – Section: Are free agents any happier?

Index